R. Bill

5 November 1935

# LANGUAGE AND LINGUISTICS
# IN THE PEOPLE'S REPUBLIC OF CHINA

An account based on the visit of
the Linguistics Delegation

October 16 to November 13, 1974

Contributors

Chin-chuan Cheng
Charles A. Ferguson
Anne FitzGerald
Victoria Fromkin
William Labov
Winfred P. Lehmann
Anatole Lyovin
John B. Lum
Frederick W. Mote
Jerry Norman
Howard E. Sollenberger
James J. Wrenn

# Language & Linguistics
# in the People's Republic of China

Edited by Winfred P. Lehmann

University of Texas Press
Austin & London

For reasons of economy and speed this volume
has been printed from camera-ready copy fur-
nished by the editor, who assumes full respon-
sibility for its contents.

International Standard Book Number 0-292-74615-6 (Cloth)
0-292-74616-4 (Paper)
Library of Congress Catalog Card Number 75-3572

# CONTENTS

## PREFACE

This book was prepared on the basis of initial essays by members of the Delegation. The names of members preparing such essays or parts of essays are not noted, on the grounds that the individual statements owe much to group discussions, in Washington, in Tokyo, and particularly in the People's Republic of China (PRC). Moreover, these essays were discussed as a whole by the entire delegation at a meeting in Washington on December 14-15, 1974. As a result many of the contributions came to be highly composite. The individual chapters then represent views of the entire delegation, not only of those members who are especially representative of a particular specialty.

Members of the delegation generally have fuller notes on the topics dealt with, particularly those topics close to their professional interests. If specific questions on any of these topics arise, they may be directed to such members, or to the Committee on Scholarly Communication with the People's Republic of China, at its Academy of Sciences address: 2101 Constitution Avenue, Washington, D.C. 20418. In this way interested readers may secure information beyond that in this book, for which compactness seemed more useful than arrays of details on each topic of linguistic concern.

Besides discussing the linguistic situation in the PRC, the book reflects means of expression widespread there. These characteristic expressions have been maintained to preserve something of the flavor of presentations made to visitors in the PRC. Among the characteristic usages, and their meanings, are:

criticize--to discuss, with an aim for improvement

divorce--separation from something worthy, as in the three divorces:--divorce from reality, from proletarian politics and from production

    popularize, popularization--spread among the people
            (NOT to cause to be liked); an increase in
            the number of people who adhere to a view or
            a practice

    practice--action, activity, application, as opposed
            to theory

    workers, peasants and soldiers or PLA──(People's
            Liberation Army)--the three major groups in-
            to which the Masses are divided in contem-
            porary China

Other terms, such as Liberation for the assumption of
power by the present government in 1949, are identified
in the text or assumed to be generally known. Like the
terms above, they give characteristic color to discussions
concerning activities in the PRC. Except for Peking, Sian,
Yenan and Canton, names of cities well known to westerners,
place names are given in pinyin without tone marks; the
background of pinyin is discussed in Chapter 3, Section 5.
Similarly, except for names which are generally cited in
western publications, such as Mao Tse-tung and Chou En-lai,
personal names are cited in pinyin. Chinese examples are
given in pinyin with tones.

As noted below, scholars in the PRC welcome exchanges
of information with Americans. Individuals sending books,
offprints and other data may not find their shipments re-
ciprocated, in  part because of differences in the patterns
of scholarly publication in the PRC, in part because of the
relatively greater costs of shipments for individuals there.
We hope that two-way communication will be made easier, and
that until it is widespread, scholars will include appropriate institutions and specialists in the PRC on their
offprint lists.

For the preparation of the book we would like to express
our appreciation to the Office of Graduate Studies of the
University of Texas at Austin for funds in support of the
preliminary and final forms, and to the American Council
of Learned Societies for funds to defray the expenses of
xeroxing the multiple copies and circulating them among
the Delegation. We would also like to thank the American
and Chinese scholars and administrators who made our visit
possible. We hope that our book as well as our visit will

lead to fuller exchanges between our country and the PRC, and also deepen the scholarly relations and the friendship of our two peoples.

# Language & Linguistics
# in the People's Republic of China

# 1. INTRODUCTION

## 1. Selection and Planning for the Delegation

This book presents the findings of the American
Linguistics Delegation which visited the People's Republic of China (PRC) from October 16 to November 13,
1974.  The Delegation was the seventh of nine to visit
China under an agreement between the Committee on Scholarly Communications with the People's Republic of China
(CSCPRC) and the National Scientific and Technical Association of the PRC in May 1973.

Initially the projected aims of the Delegation corre-
sponded to those of the English Language Study Group, a
delegation from the PRC which visited the United States
in November and December of 1973; like the English Language
Study Group, the Delegation was to focus on the study and
teaching of the host country's language.  General linguists as well as specialists in Chinese language and
linguistics were included in the Delegation.  Together
these two groups modified and determined the aims of the
Delegation.

The members of the Delegation were selected by a committee of four appointed by the CSCPRC; the Delegation
chairman was included in this committee.  All delegations
sent under the agreement with the PRC include a China
scholar whose specialty may be unrelated to that of the
delegation; the Linguistics Delegation's China scholar was
Frederick Mote.  Delegations also include a representative
of CSCPRC, who acts as secretary for the delegation;
Anne FitzGerald filled this role in the Linguistics Delegation.  Some delegations include a representative from
the Department of State; Howard Sollenberger was selected
for this position.  As a result, the selection committee

had eight participants to choose.

These eight members were: Chin-chuan Cheng, Charles A. Ferguson, Victoria Fromkin, William Labov, John Lum, Anatole Lyovin, Jerry Norman and James Wrenn. As indicated in the Notes on Contributors, they represent the specialties listed in the following paragraph. Upon the acceptance of these eight scholars a planning meeting of the members of the Delegation was scheduled. The Delegation was fortunate in having seven members who could converse in Putonghua.

At its meeting, which was held in Washington on June 26-27, the following topics were selected for study during the visit in the PRC:

1. changes in the Chinese language, and language planning, both for the spoken and written language;

2. Chinese language teaching and bilingualism;

3. language pathology and the biological basis of language;

4. lexicography;

5. non-Han languages;

6. history of the Chinese language;

7. the teaching of English and other foreign languages.

These topics, with detailed descriptions and a proposed itinerary, were sent to China's National Scientific and Technical Association in a letter of 31 July.

The initial week of activities in the PRC, as well as subsequent findings, led to modifications of these topics. For example, it soon became clear that Chinese linguists were currently carrying out little work in historical linguistics, or even in the history of the Chinese language. On the other hand, the Delegation came to be impressed with the remarkable record of the PRC in language planning. As a result, the Delegation modified its aims to reflect what it found and what it could find in the PRC. This book is structured accordingly, giving space in proportion to the current linguistic activities in the PRC as these came to be known to the Delegation.

The Delegation was also impressed by the large number of students wherever it visited. For example, Zhengzhou,

a city of approximately the same size as San Francisco
(700,000) has a student population of 170,000, in contrast
with San Francisco's 68,000.  On the other hand, the educational bureaucracy is much smaller.  Shanghai was reported
to have about 100, in contrast with San Francisco, a city
approximately one-seventeenth as large, which has about
200 persons in its educational bureaucracy.  Other general
differences were found in class size, which in the PRC
schools averages about 50 students in contrast with about
30 in American schools.  These and other findings resulted
from many meetings with Chinese students, teachers and administrators, many of whom are listed with their institu-
tional affiliations in Appendix II.  Appendix I summarizes
our itinerary.  These meetings  usually observed a standard
format.  After introduction of the participants, the hosts
would briefly describe their institution.  The Delegation
then made its observations, attending classes, visiting
laboratory installations and libraries, and the like, before meeting again to discuss the activities and programs
of the installation in question.  The greater part of each
meeting was taken up with discussions.

2.   Background on Current Education in the PRC

The discussions invariably referred to various key
events in the recent course of Chinese history, since
these events have had an important impact on education in
China.  Their significance in this context will be outlined below.

When the present government of the PRC came into power
in 1949, the event referred to hereafter as Liberation,
all educational activities were modified.  In the early
years of the PRC, Chinese education was modelled in part
after the Soviet system.  However, during the Great Proletarian Cultural Revolution, 1966-1969, a major transformation occurred.  Primary and middle school classes
were interrupted, and universities closed for several years,
while teachers and students participated in the campaign
to overcome bourgeois tendencies.  During those years new
ideas for education emerged, and were soon embodied in
the current experiment in education called the Educational
Revolution.

The Educational Revolution has focussed on five major reforms:

1.  the goals of education

2.  the enrollment system of universities

3.  teaching methods and materials

4.  examinations

5.  methods of running schools.

The goals of education today are to train students intellectually, morally, and physically, for the purpose of carrying out the Revolution.  Students are taught to analyze and solve practical problems, not to "become encyclopedias."  As Chinese teachers explain: "We put politics first; we are against putting intellectual training in the first place."  To deepen their learning and to develop their political consciousness, students "go to society and learn from the peasants, workers, and soldiers," by doing physical labor in communes, factories, or the army during the school year.

The reform of the enrollment system has focussed on enrolling more women and more students from among the workers, peasants, and soldiers.  Before the Cultural Revolution most university students came from advantaged families who by virtue of their positions in the Party or the bureaucracy could use influence to have their children enrolled in institutions of higher learning.  Today, however, about 80 percent of the university students come from the workers, peasants, and soldiers, and the balance between men and women students has greatly improved.

Under the new admissions system, most potential candidates have graduated from a five-year middle school, although some non-graduates with long experience in countryside, factory, or army have been admitted.  The selection of students involves four steps:

1.  The potential student, who is engaged in practical work at the time, applies for higher education.  He provides information on his class, education, and work background and may express his interests in a particular field of study.

2.  His work unit must endorse his application and recommend the applicant to the leaders of the commune,

factory, or military unit.

3.  The Revolutionary Committee of the larger unit reviews the candidate's qualifications, with particular attention to his class background, his potential as an active
socialist worker, and his political commitment to the socialist revolution.

4.  The educational institution must approve the
application.  Little emphasis is placed on academic background, although most institutions give either oral inter-
views or written examinations before accepting a candidate.

Teaching methods have changed to reflect a new teacher-
student relationship.  Before the Cultural Revolution
teachers viewed their job as a profession; now they teach
for the revolution.  Teachers were authoritative and
students were passive; now teachers and students have an
equal voice in determining the content and operation of
classes.  Formerly the content was highly theoretical,
but now teaching materials have been simplified, and
focus on politics and practical experience.  Application,
referred to as practice, is given high priority in the
attempts to redress the former imbalance between theory
and practice.  In addition, the length of schooling has
been cut down to five years for primary school, five years
for middle school, and three years for college.  In some
cities, such as Shanghai, primary school extends six years
and middle school only four years.

In the past, examinations were often used to terrorize
the students.  Today students are usually allowed to have
textbooks, notes, and reference materials during an exam.
Grades are awarded after discussions between students,
teachers, and workers.  In effect, examinations are given
to help students review and consolidate what they have
learned.  Exams indicate not only how well the students
are learning but also how well the teachers are teaching.

Every school is now run in the Open Door Way, a method
which takes students and teachers out into society, reducing
the concentration on  the classroom, textbook, and teacher,
and also brings members of society into the schools.  Each
school has established links with certain communes and
factories where its students are sent regularly to engage
in practical work during the school year.  The youngest
children do work around the school; the older primary

school and middle school students spend at least one month
a year doing physical labor; and university students spend
one-third of their time in workshops on the campus, in factories, or in communes.  By this method teaching is combined
with politics as well as with practice.

A recent development which has had great impact on education and on the whole society is the campaign to criticize
Lin Piao and Confucius.  Initiated in early 1974, this movement involves the rejection of the conservative authority
advocated by Confucius and indirectly, by revisionists
like Lin Piao.  Much attention is given to this campaign
in the schools; a great deal of time is now devoted to
reading and criticizing the works of Confucius, as well
as reading the theories of his opponents, the Legalists,
whose ideas are in favor.  It is explained that the Legalists advocated the transformation of society, while the
Confucianists sought the return to a Golden Age in the
past, which was actually a slave society.

To "make the past serve the present," scholars and
students are now studying the Chinese Classics critically.
Linguists are focussing particular attention on the word-
ing of the texts, reinterpreting the meaning of the
Classics through a minute analysis of the words and phrases.
The movement to criticize Lin Piao and Confucius has affected the content of teaching and linguistic research, just
as it has penetrated the whole society.

This is a brief account of the situation which the
Delegation found, of the setting in which it did its work.
The following chapters can only provide a sample of many
linguistic activities in the PRC.  Like American linguists,
Chinese linguists travel.  Some we would have liked to meet
were absent from their institutions on field trips, or they
were working in the countryside or in factories.  Though
there will accordingly be gaps in our book, we think that
our findings will be more useful if we make them available
as quickly as possible in spite of inadequacies.

In publishing this book we would like to dedicate it to
our Chinese hosts, who provided us with our data and
arranged a very informative and pleasant tour for us; and
to the American scholars who have worked so long to improve
exchanges between the people of the PRC and the people of
the USA.  Our hosts went to great pains to fulfill our
requests.  They introduced us to the life of the workers

in the cities and to the life of the peasants in the
communes.  They also acquainted us with the great past
of their country, from neolithic villages uncovered in
recent excavations through the splendors of the Tang and
other dynasties to the highlights of contemporary Chinese
culture.  Our colleagues in the universities and institutes gave us freely of their time, as did the teachers
in the middle and primary schools, and teachers in specialized schools, such as those for the deaf.  Any authority our statements may have owes much to all of them.  We
hope that our visit and our book may lead to greater cooperation between students, teachers and institutions in
our two countries.

## 2. THE COMMON LANGUAGE AND THE LANGUAGE
## OF EVERYDAY LIFE

### 1. Language and Dialect in China

This chapter presents a view of the socio-linguistic situation in China as it is reflected in the use of the newly developing common language, Putonghua. This development takes place within a larger linguistic situation of considerable complexity. The situation is similar in many ways to that which has been described in other Asian countries, such as India; see Charles A. Ferguson and John J. Gumperz (eds.) (<u>Linguistic Diversity in South Asia: Studies in Regional, Social and Functional Variation</u>. IJAL 26.3 Part III. Bloomington, Indiana, 1960). As in many other nations, there are local dialects, regional standards at several levels, and a common national standard. But the Chinese situation is unique in several respects, and many terms such as "language" and "dialect" are used in senses special to it. This first section will therefore review the relations of languages and dialects as we were informed of that situation during our trip. We will try to relate this new linguistic situation to the broader changes that are taking place in Chinese society. Throughout this presentation we will be drawing upon the rich linguistic competence of our hosts to illustrate the general tendencies we observed.

The Chinese language as a whole is most frequently referred to as <u>Zhongwen</u> though this technically applies to the written as opposed to the spoken language (<u>Zhongguo hua</u>). Ninety-four percent of the Chinese people are said to speak "Han language" (<u>Hanyu</u>). Within this category there are two major sub-categories: (1) the common or standard language, Putonghua, and (2) all others, which

are referred to as "dialects," fang yan.  Putonghua was defined and endorsed at the Standardization Conference of
October, 1955, as the common language of the PRC, embodying
the pronunciation of the general Peking dialect, the grammar
of Northern Chinese dialects, and the vocabulary of modern
colloquial Chinese literature.  The dialects were usually
organized for us by Chinese scholars into eight major groups.
These are more different from each other than Spanish and
Italian, and some perhaps more different than French and
Italian.  Most of the major groups are mutually unintelligible for speakers who have had no past history of contact with the other variety.  The largest number of people
speak Northern dialects (Mandarin) in the north, northwest, west and southwest, of which Peking is taken as the
exemplar.  In the East, a large population, including
Shanghai, speak Wu dialects.  The most different and the
most highly differentiated dialects are in the southeast,
where Cantonese, Fukienese, Hakka, etc. offer the most
difficulty for speakers of other dialects.
     Within each dialect area many subdivisions can be made
on a purely geographical basis, again with the greatest
degree of diversity in the southeast.  There are also regional standards or more formal varieties in each area.
We do not observe a typical three-level hierarchy of standard, regional standard and local dialects, but rather a
series of formal and informal dimensions at each geographic
subdivision accompanied by bilingual competence in the
common language, Putonghua.  We can illustrate the complexity of linguistic repertoires in China by drawing on
the competence of a staff member of the Chinese People's
Association for Friendship with Foreign Countries who
accompanied us throughout our trip and did much of the work
of interpreting.  He was born in Ningbo, a small city not
far from Shanghai, and grew up speaking Ningbo dialect.
He lived in Shanghai for several years, and therefore
knows the Shanghai dialect quite well.  For many years
he has lived in Peking, used Putonghua in his work, and
traveled across the country with many delegations.  He
is therefore more widely traveled than most Chinese people.
He is quite interested in language, and in some ways is a
linguistic virtuoso.  His multidialectal strengths and
weaknesses illustrate the dynamics of the sociolinguistic
situation in China.

We may take a sentence such as "Where did you go to
play [for recreation]?"  We can contrast four varieties
in a broad phonetic transcription, three of them available to this speaker:

Putonghua ["standard" Peking pronunciation]

[ni taɔ ʂəm·a tifaŋ tɕʰü war lə]

Putonghua [his pronunciation]

[ni dɔ səm·a difã tɕʰü wɛr lə]

Shanghai, informal

[nɔŋ dɔʔ sa difã tɕʰι ba ɕiɛ tɕʰι lə]

Ningbo, informal

[nɔŋ dɔʔ soᵘ difã tɕʰι naŋoᵘ tɕʰι lə]

The differences in the pronunciation of Putonghua are
quite typical of those we observed thoughout our trip,
and will be discussed below.  Shanghai and Ningbo both
differ in the form of the pronouns: nong instead of ni
for the second person singular, and both use a completely different word for 'play': ba ɕiɛ in Shanghai, and
naŋoᵘ in Ningbo.  The personal pronouns themselves are
among the most diagnostic features of the dialectal contrasts, and illustrate the way in which the formal varieties of the dialects approach the standard.

|  | Putonghua | formal Shanghai Ningbo | informal Shanghai | informal Ningbo |
|---|---|---|---|---|
| 1st sg. | wɔ | ŋou | ŋənou | ŋənou |
| 2nd sg. | ni | ni | nɔŋ | nɔŋ |
| 3rd sg. | ta | ta | yiləʔ | ji |

In the course of our trip, this staff member was frequently called on to translate other dialects, when some of our
hosts or guides spoke in the local dialects at our request
in Sian, Suzhou, and Linxian.  He was also tested by varieties of Putonghua which were heavily influenced by local
dialects, and he handled them without hesitation.  But he
freely admitted that most of the southeastern dialects,

including Cantonese, were too hard for him to handle.

Though this speaker was sensitive to variation in lexicon and grammatical particles, he was not at all sensitive to many phonetic differences, and used his own Ningbo
phonetics and phonology in both Chinese and English.  To
be sure we heard many Chinese who had mastered the phonetics of Peking style Putonghua; but they proved to be a
very special sub-set of speakers (see Section 4.3), and
this speaker's pattern was quite typical of many Chinese
in leading positions as well as factory workers and peasants.

It is often said that this phonetic freedom is toler-
able in Putonghua and does not lead to misunderstanding.
But we observed many examples of semantic confusion resul-
ting from it which produced real problems of misunder-
standings (see Section 4.1).  Furthermore, Chinese scholars
frequently cited anecdotes which illustrated the problems
that result from dialect interference.  One such instance
was cited to us from a letter to the newspaper from a PLA
man: an order to examine the telegraph lines was trans-
mitted as an order to pull down the telegraph lines, and
carried out!  It is also commonly said that many Chinese
have the polydialectal competence that we illustrated
above but against these statements are to be weighed the
repeated arguments for popularizing Putonghua, such as
this incident reported to us at Fudan University.

> At present, the whole countryside is learning
> from Dazhai Brigade, so many peasants go there.
> When Chen Yong-gui, the Brigade leader, gave a
> report to them, some peasants from Fukien province
> could not understand what he was saying, no matter
> how excellent his speech was, so it had to be trans-
> lated into a number of different dialects.

In characterizing the overall sociolinguistic situation,
the Chinese emphasize the inability of speakers to understand each other rather than the degree of polylectal competence which is found.  From the data given above, it can
readily be seen that the formal varieties of the local
dialects are closer to Putonghua.  In most countries, it
would follow that literacy would automatically bring the
dialects closer to the standard.  But in China the rapid
growth of literacy does not have this effect, since the

same written language is used for all Han dialects.

Although the sociolinguistic situation in China shows
great diversity, it is less diversified than other areas,
such as India, in three respects:

(1)  The great majority of the dialects spoken are
members of one language family rather than two or more.

(2)  A single script and writing system can be used
for all of these related languages.

(3)  A single language, or group of dialects, is
spoken by a majority of Chinese and is therefore a reason-
able candidate for a standard language.

If we are to assess the full consequences of this situation, it must be seen against the larger social background of the Chinese revolution, and the conflicts in
Chinese society which remain to be resolved.  The changes
of recent history were summed up for us by Chinese spokesmen in the following way.

Before Liberation, the Chinese people had been
oppressed by imperialism, bureaucratic capitalism, and the
remnants of feudalism; after Liberation, the proletariat
has become the leading class, and the laboring people
have become the masters of the country.  The proletarian
revolution aims at eliminating the exploiting classes
and the system of exploitation step by step, and finally
eliminating classes altogether.  Yet according to Chairman Mao, there are still classes, class contradictions,
and class struggle in the present period of building socialism.  Since 1949, the Chinese people have waged a
series of struggles against the bourgeoisie and its agents
in the Communist Party.  The Great Proletarian Cultural
Revolution which began in 1966 is a test of strength between the proletariat and the remaining forces of the
bourgeoisie.  The current movement to criticize Lin Piao
and Confucius is a continuation of the political and ideological struggle of the Cultural Revolution.

When the new social system was established in 1949, the
Chinese language was at first unaffected.  In the view of
dialectical materialism, language is a product of the whole
society and serves all social classes; it is not a part
of the ideological superstructure erected by the ruling
class.  Nevertheless, three major changes in the linguistic

situation have occurred since Liberation.

(1)   The national development of China requires a
rationalization of the language system.  A unified script
exists, but the technical and educational drawbacks of the
character system represent a serious drain on the time
and energy of the society.  A romanized alphabet would
solve this problem, but such a phonetic alphabet for
Putonghua will only be practical when all Chinese have
access to a single spoken language.  This need existed
before Liberation, but corruption and lack of ability
to mobilize the people made any serious progress impossible.
Today the drive for universal access to Putonghua is the
key to solving the language problems of modern China.

(2)   The social changes of the past twenty-five years
have brought forth a host of new conditions, and since
language is a means of social communication, this has
brought about socially significant changes in the Chinese
language.  New words have come into use and old words
have disappeared or been sharply modified in meaning (see
Section 4.1).

(3)   The new social conditions have created a need for
drastic changes in the style of expression in Chinese
literature and speech.  The language policy of the Communist Party and Chairman Mao's directives have urged that
this style be changed to fit the new social situation where
the models for emulation are drawn from the workers and
peasants rather than from ancient writers, the bourgeoisie,
the intelligentsia, or foreign cultures.  In his 1942 article, "Oppose Stereotyped Party Writing," Chairman Mao
called for party members to study colloquial language.

> First, let us learn language from the masses.
> The people's vocabulary is rich, vigorous,
> vivid and expressive of real life.... Second,
> let us absorb what we need from foreign lan-
> guages.  We should not import foreign expres-
> sions mechanically or use them indiscriminate-
> ly, but should absorb what is good and what
> suits our needs... Third, let us also learn
> whatever is alive in the classical Chinese lan-
> guage.

Given the need for change in the language situation,
one might expect a series of decrees changing the vocabulary, outlawing dialects, and so on.  But the Chinese
approach to effecting social change is basically one of
persuasion and mobilizing social opinion.  They believe
that social change, and linguistic change, must be accom-
plished at the level of primary social organization.  In
the campaign to popularize language policy among the
masses, major newspapers such as the <u>People's Daily</u> have
played a significant role, but many other forms of social
organization are mobilized.

In the Chinese situation, we then observe two types of
factors working side by side: social realities and language policy.  A socially significant but artificial mo-
dification in the language, which does not reflect social
reality, may not succeed in obtaining widespread usage.
On the other hand, the Chinese believe that their language will not develop in the right direction and at the
right speed to meet the new social developments, without
deliberate effort and proper guidance.  In the next section of this chapter, we will present the goals of Chinese
society as they were formulated for us by the Chinese
spokesmen.  The larger issues of national language reform
will be developed in the discussion of language reform in
Chapter 3.  Here we will be concerned with the consequences
for the use of language in day-to-day communication through
the rapidly developing common language.  We will then
proceed to discuss the place of linguistic research in
that program (Section 3); present current observations on
the state of the common language by Chinese linguists as
well as ourselves (Section 4); and finally, attempt to
evaluate the progress made in reaching these goals (Section 5).

2.  Goals Set by the Chinese People for the Use of

      Putonghua

2.1  The Relation of Dialects to the Common Language

Plans for the popularization of Putonghua do not call
for immediate elimination of local dialects.  In answer
to questions on the policy towards the ultimate status
of dialects, it was frequently repeated to us that dialects

will not die out for a long time.  At the same time, there
seems to be some variation in fundamental attitude towards
this question.  No one who discussed the matter stated in
so many words that there were any positive values in linguistic pluralism.  And some strategies of dialectologists
seem to imply a policy of engineering the dialects out of
existence (see Section 3.2).  In line with the fundamental
position on the relations of theory and practice, the
Chinese seem unwilling to speculate on this abstract question.
But given the practical position of the Committee on Language Reform that "dialects cannot be abolished by administrative order," and that "dialects are useful for communication in certain areas," it follows that "cadres should
learn local dialects to develop closer contacts with the
masses."  The Chinese linguists expect to see interaction
between dialects and Putonghua for a long time to come.

## 2.2  What Kind of Common Language?

As defined by official policy, Putonghua is a language
with pronunciation based on the Peking dialect, the grammar
of the northern dialects, and the lexicon of modern literary Chinese.  Beyond these formal requirements, it is
hoped that under the new social conditions, the vocabulary
and style of this new common language will be close to the
language of working people in the communes and the factories, and not become a diglossic standard language remote from the language of everyday life.  This goal was
articulated for us most explicitly in our visit to a high
school (Middle School #15) in Peking.  In the course of
explaining how the Open Door Way was applied in this school,
the Chinese teacher explained that students

> go to the factories as well as the countryside to
> integrate with the peasants and workers, to learn
> from their rich language... We think that the
> peasants' and workers' language is very vivid
> and rich, and our teachers' language is really
> a bit bookish...

This goal was further illustrated for us by Mr. Mao
Cheng-dong, a teacher at the Peking Language Institute.
He concluded his lecture on "The development of the Chinese
vocabulary" by analyzing the writings of Chairman Mao.

He described Chairman Mao's style as "creative, brilliant,
and fresh," and also quoted Chairman Mao's statement that
"the language of the working people is our most valuable
resource."

The goal of correcting literary style, and learning
from everyday language, is continued in higher education.
At Shanghai Normal University, one of our hosts told us
how students in their study of contemporary Chinese literature applied the principle of going to the countryside
to learn from peasants and workers.  While studying the
Peking Opera "On the Docks," they went to the dock area
of Shanghai, and wrote papers discussing how the operatic
language had been shifted to reflect the language that
dock workers actually use, at the same time maintaining
the "compressed, elevated" style of the art form.

It was continually emphasized that this common language
should be heavily informed by political thinking and reflect a correct political line.  It is important to note
that in China politics and propaganda are positive terms.
Where an American might criticize the style of a speech
or a lecture as being "too political" or as containing
"too much propaganda," this criticism would not be coherent
within the modern Chinese framework, where it is believed
that the political line reflects the everyday thinking
and life-experience of the common people.

2.3  The Use of Language in the Classroom

Since the role of linguistics in education was a central concern of our delegation, we had many discussions
of the use of language in the classroom, and observed
Putonghua being used in a number of schools.  The Cultural
Revolution set new goals for linguistic behavior in this
area.  Classroom behavior before 1966 is said to have been
strongly influenced by Russian practice, which reinforced
the traditional Chinese system of strict discipline, group
repetition of the teachers' words and rote learning.  The
current goals of Chinese education are to encourage free
discussion at all levels, to reduce the extreme respect
for the teacher which prevented students from speaking up.
The movement to criticize Lin Piao and Confucius has
attacked authoritarian principle which elevated the teacher
over the student.

Throughout China, it is a very important political goal
that Putonghua be used as the medium of instruction in the
classroom.  But since students are expected to speak up
freely, report their own experiences, and criticize teachers
as well as their fellow students, it is clear that a very
high level of linguistic competence is expected.  If the
students were only required to develop passive interpre-
tive abilities, and respond in brief, correct answers,
the task of teaching Putonghua would obviously be a much
simpler one.  If we combine the expectations of (1) a
rich, vivid language with (2) free and critical expression,
we see that the goals set for the use of Putonghua are quite
high.

In the universities, the achievement of the first goal
may have been facilitated by the radical change in the
composition of the student body brought about by the Cultural Revolution.  In each of the universities we visited,
it was said that most of the students are now drawn from
workers' and peasants' families.  In any event, all students will have been exposed to the language of the countryside and factory for several years after high school,
regardless of their family or class background.

In most areas, the use of Putonghua to express the life
experience of working people will require an exercise in
translation.  At the Cao Yang 1st Primary School in Shanghai, we were told that students in Chinese classes went
out to interview older workers in the city, and wrote
papers reporting their life experiences.  The student then
read his paper to the man he interviewed, and a mark was
given by the person interviewed, the teacher, and the students.  The normal situation would be that an older working
man would be speaking in Shanghai dialect, and the student
would read his written paper in Putonghua.  For a Shanghai
student, there would be no direct model for this kind of
expression in Putonghua, and he would therefore have to
create his own model.

As part of the Open Door Way, workers and peasants are
often invited to the schools to lecture to the students.
We did not hear any of these lectures, but the expectation
is that they would be delivered in Putonghua.  An older
worker would then have the same task of translating his
everyday experience into Putonghua, and there would be
many pressures to develop the capacity for expression in
the standard language.

## 3. The Place of Research in the Study of Everyday Language

### 3.1 Relation of Theory and Practice

In all discussions of linguistic theory, Chinese linguists emphasized their basic position, that (1) theory must be combined with practice, and (2) practice comes first. In an informal exchange with linguists from the Central Institute for Nationalities, we put forward the position that it was possible to study an applied problem and a basic theoretical problem at the same time, and that American researchers found it important to ask fundamental questions of "Why?" and "How?" The Chinese linguists argued that theory grows from practice, and only in the struggle to solve practical problems would a correct theory emerge.

This problem of the relations of theory and practice was put in a broader perspective by Zhou Pei-yuan, the Vice-chairman of the Revolutionary Committee at Peking University, one of the leading spokesmen in academic life.

> Since China is a backward country, we must first develop agriculture and industry to raise our living standards. But basic theory is very important, and we cannot look down upon it. In some scientific research, some basic theory might not have immediate practical use, but will be very useful in the future. There are many examples in the sciences of physics and biology which had no immediate application but proved very important in the long run. How much time should be spent on theoretical research, and how much time should be spent on the applications of theory is a question of scientific planning. Generally speaking, we emphasize research on theory which has a close connection with present-day national economic development. This is true not only in China but also throughout the world; it is the same in the United States. In connection with theoretical research, many problems are being solved in the factories and the countryside. Most problems come from industry and

   agriculture, but still we spend part of our
   effort on fundamental research.  For example,
   in our department of physics, we have a group
   on theoretical physics, and that group is interested in the investigation of fundamental
   particles; elementary particle physics is,
   you know, rather abstract and basic.  Now of
   course I know little about linguistics,...
   but I think that theoretical research in linguistics must be going on while we are popularizing Putonghua in the whole country--that
   must be based on theoretical work.

Thus we see from this statement that in the overall
perspective, the Chinese attitude towards the relations
of theory and practice does not differ radically from ours.
But given the immediate situation, China does differ from
the United States in its concentration on a unified set of
national goals, and the subordination of specific sciences
to those goals.  Whereas the need for basic research in
particle physics has been proved, the same cannot be said
for linguistics; the Chinese are not yet convinced that
basic research into the structure and evolution of language
has been proved to be so important that national development cannot proceed without it.

In our discussion with members of the Central Institute
for Nationalities, the unification of the Chinese approach
was strikingly contrasted with the diversification of American linguistics.  Professor Fei Xiao-tong put the question
to us quite directly: the immediate goal of Chinese linguistics is the popularization of Putonghua.  What was the
goal of American linguistics?  The great difference between China and America is therefore not the relation of
theory and practice, but unity versus diversity.

## 3.2  Research on Chinese Dialects

In line with the goals outlined above, Chinese dialectology is currently carried on in relation to the goal of
spreading and facilitating the use of Putonghua.  In
1958-1959, a nation-wide program for studying Chinese dialects was carried out in a very short time, with the aim
of charting the differences which would produce difficulties

for speakers of other dialects learning Putonghua. No
further projects seem to have been carried out until recently; and during the Cultural Revolution, work on dialectology stopped entirely. We encountered new beginnings
of dialect research at four places:

(1) At Peking University, a group of students working
under Professors Yuan Jia-hua and Wang Fu-tang, is inves-
tigating a group of dialects in Shaoshan (Chairman Mao's
birthplace), Hunan Province.

(2) At Fudan University, in Shanghai, Professor
Xu Bao-hua has been developing new research on Shanghai
dialects.

(3) At Shanghai Normal University, Professor Yan
Yi-ming of the Department of Chinese, who participated
in the study of Jiangxu dialects in 1959, plans to continue
research in the suburbs in the Shanghai area.

(4) At Zhongshan (Sun Yat-sen) University, in Canton,
Professor Huang Jia-jiao has been carrying out research on
Cantonese dialects.

At Zhongshan, we were told that no central study was
now being conducted of the 1958-1959 materials, which were
stored in county seats and also collected at Peking. Peking
University has issued two important collections which
summarize the data for a limited number of dialects: the
Hanyu Fangyin Zihui (1962) and the Hanyu Fangyan Cihui
(1964). The former is the original basis for the Dictionary
on Computer which William Wang and his associates in the
United States have used for studies of sound change in
Chinese.
Linguists at Zhongshan University told us that the dialect materials in that area were not yet ready for publication, and that at least the Cantonese materials, and
perhaps those of other areas as well, might have to be re-
assessed if they are to be used as the basis for further
work. Although the 1958 materials concentrated largely
on phonetics, they were done by field workers who received
only a short course in phonetic transcription.
Current work in Chinese dialectology is based on intimate association between researchers and speakers of the
dialects. In the Peking University field work, the students

selected poor and lower middle peasants as informants, over
a wide range of ages, and lived with their subjects during
the twenty days of field work.  In this type of research,
the dialectologists feel that they are carrying out the
goal of putting theory into practice, and overcoming the
divorce from working people and social reality.  At the
same time, the actual techniques used are still quite formal, basically devoted to obtaining the informants' pronunciations of a long list of isolated words.  The twenty
students worked with eleven informants.  Two students transcribed the pronunciation of each informant, obtaining the
pronunciation of 3,000 characters and several dozens of
sentences.

At Shanghai Normal University, the field workers hold
discussions with informants.  The subject of the discussion
is the pronunciation of the words being studied.  The field
workers do not use tape recorders, but feel that they can
get most accurate results by writing down the phonetic
transcription as the subject pronounces the words.

It is generally agreed that these formal methods may be
necessary as first steps in charting a dialect, and establishing the development of the historical word classes which
make it possible to relate the dialect to others.  The purpose of the study is contrastive analysis: to write the rules
which a speaker of a given dialect must use in order to convert his phonological system to that of Putonghua.  For
example, Professor Xu of Fudan University was concerned
with the rules which relate the four-tone system of
Putonghua with the five-tone system of the Shanghai dialects.
This subject is conventionally approached from a historical
point of view: tracing the path of the Middle Chinese tones
in each dialect.  But the present task of promoting the
popularization of Putonghua requires that these tone relations be examined from a synchronic viewpoint, examining
what a Shanghai dialect speaker without any knowledge of
linguistic history must do to convert his system to
Putonghua.

To begin with, there are two entering tones (high and
mid) in the Shanghai dialect which occur in syllables ending in voiceless stops.  Putonghua does not have such
stops, and these tones do not correspond in any systematic
way with Putonghua tones in the corresponding syllables.
The remaining three tones have to be mapped against the

four Putonghua tones.  The first (high falling) tone,
corresponds to the Putonghua high level tone.  But words
with the second (low rising) tone in Shanghai are found
with both the second (high rising) and fourth (high falling) tone in Putonghua; and words with the third (high
rising) tone in Shanghai are found with both the third
(falling-rising) and fourth (falling) tone in Putonghua.

```
                Putonghua          Shanghai
       Tone        1 ———————————————— 1
                   2 ———————————⟍  ⟋— 2
                   3 ————————⟍⟋———— 3
                   4 ⟋———————
```

With our present knowledge of the dialect, we cannot see
how a Shanghai speaker can predict when to use the Putonghua
fourth tone.  But current research being carried on in Shanghai and the suburbs may very well uncover complicated systems which would point the way to such predictions, and
help speakers of these dialects learn the Putonghua tone
system.

The research in Hunan is also aimed at uncovering the
rules of correspondence between dialects and Putonghua.
This area includes both Mandarin dialects and less closely related dialects outside of the Mandarin group.  Professor Wang Fu-tang and his Peking University students
have observed changes taking place in these dialects as
they influence each other.  From consideration of the internal changes in the relations in the dialects, they believe that a strategy of popularizing Putonghua first in
one area, Shaoshan, will lead to further changes in the
dialect which will bring it closer to others, narrowing
the gap between the dialects and Putonghua.  Professor
Wang Fu-tang summarized their overall approach to prag-
matic applications of research:

> We should not only find out the rules, but use
> the rules to change the objective world.

Linguists at Zhongshan University were also concerned
with effecting social changes through linguistic studies.
At present, Cantonese dialect plays a recognized and major
role in the mass media of the area.  There are broadcasts

in both Cantonese and Putonghua.  Linguists have noted
that in many instances there are variant forms within
Cantonese, one more similar to Putonghua than the other.
For example, the term 'blue-green' in Cantonese is pronounced either [tʃʰiŋ] or [tʃʰɛŋ]; the former is closer
to the Putonghua form [tɕʰiŋ], and it is suggested that
this be used in Cantonese broadcasts.  More important, the
Putonghua forms of the pronouns tāmen 'they' and wǒde 'my'
are both popular reading pronunciations and can be used
in broadcasting to help narrow the gap between Cantonese
and Putonghua.  The dialect repertoire of one of our hosts
reported in Section 1 shows that the same situation exists
in Shanghai and Ningbo.
    We therefore see that wherever dialect research is being
carried out, linguists are making serious efforts to apply
their knowledge to the major goals of Chinese society, and
making progress towards those goals.
    Some Chinese linguists are also conscious of the need
to study the use of language in everyday life.  At Fudan
University, Professor Xu told us that he has begun to
study the daily spoken language of a suburb of Shanghai;
but we did not have the opportunity to obtain a more detailed account of the methods he is developing.  At
Zhongshan University, Professor Huang and others seem to
have acquired a deep knowledge of the phonetics of rapid
speech, and have been following the development of the
vernacular with some attention.  But as yet there is no
systematic program for recording this material.
    The study of the Chinese language is therefore concen-
trated on fairly specific goals, devoted to establishing
basic rules of correspondence between dialects and Putonghua.
We did not encounter any program of systematic research
aimed at a better understanding of the use of language, or
recording the rich and vivid language of workers and peasants.
But it must be emphasized that Chinese linguistic activity
is highly decentralized at present, and it is quite possible
that such work is being done at centers we did not visit.

## 3.3  The Relation of Lexicology to Everyday Speech

    The decentralization of Chinese linguistics is quite
evident in the studies of the lexicon which we encountered.
At the Peking Language Institute, Mr. Mao Cheng-dong gave

us a rich account of the recent development of the vocabulary, apparently based on his personal observations
(see Section 4.1).  At Fudan University, Professor Li
Zhen-lin gave us an account of work with the Hanyu Zidian,
and with the Workers, Peasants and Soldiers Dictionary
(see Chapter 6 on Lexicography).  In the latter dictionary,
a major effort was made to incorporate words that are used
by the masses, as well as changing definitions to fit in
with the new social conditions and new uses (see Section 4.1
and Chapter 6.4).  The editors made use of their participation in the May 7th schools, where cadres work in the
countryside alongside peasants, applying their observations
there to enrich the new dictionary.  At Peking, we were
told that the Hanyu Zidian was reviewed by a very large
number of workers and peasants, as well as linguists, and
that new material was freely supplied to supplement the
older lists.

A crucial question concerns the adoption of new words
in Putonghua.  These would often be drawn from the other
Chinese dialects.  Since they would at first be local
rather than nationally known words, it would seem that the
importation of dialect words would interfere with the main
function of Putonghua to be a medium of wider communication.
At the Peking Language Institute, Mr. Mao Cheng-dong expressed the view that widespread adoption of local words
into Putonghua should be severely limited in the future,
though it had been quite widespread in the past.  It is
not clear just how such borrowings would be prevented, if
Putonghua is not to be a prescribed standard but a popular
means of expression.  Linguists from Fudan University discussed this issue with us in some detail.  How is it determined that a new colloquial term has entered Putonghua?
The process of standardization is quite obvious if the
term is widely used in the literature, or used by such
prominent writers as Chairman Mao or Lu Hsun.  But the
Chinese linguists were not willing to limit themselves to
the criterion of literary usage.  Professor Xu Bao-hua
stated that it would be necessary to investigate whether
or not the masses were widely using the term, and adopt it
in a dictionary if it had become general enough.

It was also stated that in a dictionary of Putonghua,
words could be labeled as "colloquial," "regional," or
even "slang."  It thus appears that Putonghua is not

conceived of as a rigid fixed standard, but will have considerable flexibility even in dictionaries.  The attitude
of Chinese scholars towards all such questions is quite
moderate and the tendency is to avoid prescription by rule
whenever possible.  There is a strong commitment to follow
popular practice.  At the same time, there is not yet any
systematic research to observe and describe that practice.

    In a discussion at Peking University, linguists re-
sponded to this question by considering favorably the
possibility that more Chinese linguistic research might undertake observation of verbal interaction in a way similar
to the techniques developed in American sociolinguistics.
It is clear that more resources are available in China for
such study, under more favorable conditions, than in the
United States.  But it is also clear that if Chinese dialectology begins again on a large scale, first priority
will be given to the collection of word-level data with
formal word lists.

## 4.   Observations of the Chinese Language

### 4.1   Observations of the Changing Vocabulary

    In our visits to Chinese universities, we were given
many rich and penetrating observations on changes in the
Chinese vocabulary under the impact of new social conditions.  We will be drawing heavily upon these observations
in the following discussion, as well as our own.  In particular, we will be utilizing a lecture of Mr. Mao Cheng-dong,
of the Peking Language Institute, on "The Development of the
Chinese Vocabulary after the Establishment of the People's
Republic," which has since been published in the Journal
of Chinese Linguistics (Vol. 2, No. 3, 1974) as one of
the first scholarly exchanges which resulted from our trip.

    As the socialist system developed, some of the ideas
of the old ruling classes disappeared, and the corresponding linguistic expressions disappeared with them.  Before Liberation, the basic terms for address for upper
class women were tài tai ('madam') and xiǎo jie ('miss'),
and these terms are still taught in introductory texts
published in the United States.  Both have been dropped
from general use in modern China, as they reflected respect
for the elite status held by the gentry in the past.  Today

they are used only in a derogatory sense to refer to someone who shows, in the Chinese view, remnants of elitist
thinking or behavior. [The term xiǎo jie is still used
without a derogatory sense to address unmarried foreign
females, and was used to a member of our delegation.]

In this regard the teaching of Chinese in the United
States has not kept up with the Chinese language develo-
ment in China. In the PRC the word xiān sheng may mean
'teacher', 'medical doctor', or 'mister'. But it is now
rarely used for the first two meanings. In diplomatic
circles it is used to mean 'Mr.'. In the USA the word
is taught to mean 'Mr.', 'teacher', or 'husband'.

As such words are eliminated, new words appear, to
fulfill the new functions. In China tóng zhì 'comrade',
which was originally used to refer to party comrades, is
now used to address others as well. In everyday life more
intimate expressions such as lǎo Chén 'old buddy Chen',
xiǎo Wǔ 'little old buddy Wu', or simply names are used.

In the old society, honorific expressions such as the
following were common:

| | |
|---|---|
| gùi shěng | 'your honorable province' |
| bǐ chù | 'my humble place' |
| lǐng zūn | 'your honorable father' |
| lǐng táng | 'your honorable mother' |

We were told that all such expressions today were considered nonsensical, and we did not observe any being used.
They are replaced by such straightforward literal expressions
as nǐde fùchin, 'your father'.

The egalitarian spirit manifests itself especially on
job descriptions. Old terms describing a person's occupation with derogatory meanings have been replaced by positive names, for example:

| old name | meaning | new name |
|---|---|---|
| huǒ fū | cook in a military unit | chuī shì yuán |
| nóng fū | peasant | shè yuán |
| mǎ fū | animal caretaker | sì yǎng yuán |
| chē fū | driver | jià shì yuán |

| old name | meaning | new name |
|----------|---------|----------|
| yóu chāi | mailman | yóu dī yuán |
| tīng chāi | attendant | fú wù yuán |
| lǎo mā zi | nurse--amah | bǎo yù yuán |
| kǔ lì | worker | gōng rén |

The term fū literally means 'man', but in these combina-
tions it has a strong connotation of 'lowly' or 'inferior'
person. Chāi refers to a person who runs errands for others.
The expression lǎo mā zi refers to a dependent role that
no longer exists in Chinese society. Finally the term
kǔ lì (literally, 'bitter strength') is the source of
English coolie, which symbolizes more than any other term
the former oppression and degradation of the working class.
All of these terms of reference to working people are now
replaced by yuán, 'member' or rén, 'human being', which are
associated with the most dignified and respected roles in
Chinese society; cf. shè yuán, 'commune member', and gōng
rén, 'factory worker'.
   The name of the city Dí huà in Xinjiang has been changed
back to the original name Wū lǔ mù qí, 'flower city'. The
words Dí huà meaning 'to be enlightened and culturalized'
are considered an insult to the civilization of the Uighur
people. The city in the Inner Mongolia Autonomous Region,
Guī Suí, which literally means 'to be Chinese-civilized'
has been changed back to the original name hū hé hào tè,
which in Mongolian means 'blue city'.
   The new role of women in Chinese society is exemplified
by Chairman Mao's saying: "Women can hold up half of the
sky." So bàn biān tiān 'half of the sky' is now a synonym
for 'woman'. Āiren 'beloved--spouse' has replaced the sex-
discriminatory terms wài zǐ 'outside person--husband' and
nèi rén 'inside person--wife' or jiàn nèi 'humble inside--
wife'. In the old society one heard the expression lǎo bù
sǐ de 'the old man who dies hard'— meaning 'husband'. By
contrast, in Shanghai we heard an old woman refer to her
husband as lǎo àiren 'the old beloved'.
   The influence of classical Chinese on the colloquial
language is rapidly diminishing. Chinese majors in universities are not required to be able to write in classical
Chinese, even though writings in classical Chinese such as

those by Confucianists and Legalists are extensively read
during the current movement to criticize Lin Piao and Confucius.  In the past, classical Chinese was considered
especially appropriate for inscriptions on gravestones.
Yet today we find simple colloquial language, such as the
one which we read on the grave of Edgar Snow at Peking
University:

   Zhōngguó rénmínde Měiguó péngyou Āīdéjiā Sinuò zhī mù

which was translated "In memory of Edgar Snow, an American
friend of the Chinese people."  If this inscription had
shown the influence of classical Chinese, it would not have
the modern colloquial possessive particle de or the term
péngyou, 'friend', but simply yǒu embodied in some more
poetic and elliptical expression.  A typical classical
inscription, for example, is Yīng liè qiān qiū; four characters which literally mean 'hero,' 'martyr,' 'thousand,'
'autumn,' and might be interpreted to mean 'May this hero's
memory remain for a thousand years.'
   There is a strong tendency in modern Chinese for the
drastic shortening of commonly used phrases, particularly
those which are widespread through their use in political
discussions.  The following idioms using the number sān,
'three', would be quite opaque to Chinese speakers who had
not been in touch with recent developments.

   sān tuō lí      'three divorces' used instead of 'di-
                   vorced from reality, proletarian poli-
                   tics and production'

   sān zhōng xīn   'three centers' instead of 'take the
                   textbook, classroom, and teacher as
                   the centers for learning'

   sān jié hé      'three combines' instead of 'combina-
                   tion of the old, middle-aged, and young,
                   etc.'

   sān dà gémìng yùndòng
                   'three great revolutionary movements' in-
                   stead of 'struggle for production, class
                   struggle, and scientific experiment'

   Over the past 25 years, many new institutions have
arisen through the revolutionary changes that have taken

place in society.  As a result we find many newly created
phrases for referring to them:

| | |
|---|---|
| hóng wèi bīng | 'red guard' |
| tiě gūniang | 'iron girl' |
| chì jiǎo yī shēng | 'barefoot doctor' |
| gé mìng wěi yuán huì | 'revolutionary committee' |
| wǔ qī gàn xiào | 'May 7th cadre school' |
| gōng nóng bīng xué yuán | 'worker-peasant-soldier stu-dents--college students' |
| kāi mén bàn xué | 'running schools in an Open Door Way' |
| pī Lín pī Kǒng | 'to criticize Lin Piao and Confucius' |

## 4.2  Dialect Influences on Putonghua

   During our trip through China, we were able to observe
Putonghua spoken by a wide variety of speakers, including
professors, officials, peasants, and working people.  In
each visit to a school, factory, or farm, we were introduced to the situation by a leading member of the Revolutionary Committee, and were able to record his speech in
a formal statement as well as less formal discussions.
We also recorded speech from less prominent people, such
as residents of local neighborhoods and peasants.  When
we visited a family in a commune, it was to be expected
that the speakers selected to meet us would usually be
practiced at meeting visitors, and selected because they
best represented the norms of the society.  But since
two-thirds of our delegation spoke Chinese, it was possible to make many other observations of the use of local
dialects and Putonghua.  Though our schedule was quite
crowded with official trips, we were able to walk freely
through the streets in the morning and evening, and there
was no restraint put upon our movements within the city
we were visiting.  Several of our members were able to
conduct long conversations with local speakers, in some
instances meeting working people who were encountered

without any plan or introduction by our hosts.  We were
also able to make some rough assessment of the use of
Putonghua versus local dialects in a number of cities we
visited.  At the same time, it should be emphasized that
our observations were brief and unsystematic, subject to
the bias of many accidents, and cannot substitute for the
detailed study of everyday language which we hope the
Chinese linguists will undertake.  Our most systematic
data comes from thirty to forty hours of recorded formal
speeches in Putonghua spoken by members of Revolutionary
Committees, professors, teachers, archeologists, museum
guides, and informants selected by our hosts.  Within this
framework, we can make some preliminary observations about
dialect influences on the common language, and in future
reports we will be able to present more detailed accounts
of the sociolinguistic variables in Putonghua.  These preliminary observations will concentrate on the main phonological variables.
    (N):  One of the most prominent variables concerns the
behavior of final nasals.  As W. S-Y. Wang and C. C. Cheng
(Implementation of phonological change: the Shuang-feng
Chinese case.  Papers for the Sixth Regional Meeting —
Chicago Linguistic Society, pp. 552-559, 1970) point out,
Chinese dialects can be organized in a series by their
relative degree of advance in the general process of loss
of final consonants.  In general, the final stops /p t k/
are glottalized and then lost before the final nasals are
lost.  In the Peking dialect, final stops have all disappeared, but the system distinguishes two points of nasal
articulation: /n/ versus /ŋ/ in syllable-final position.
For low vowels, there is a clear difference in quality
before the two nasals, with a backer vowel before /ŋ/, so
that the distinctive difference need not be carried by the
consonant.  But for some other dialects, there is little
phonetic difference for some vowels before /n/ and /ŋ/,
and mergers of similar forms can result.  The standard
Peking dialect is marked by the oral quality of the vowels
before nasals, and clear pronunciation of the finals /n/
and /ŋ/.  Since other dialects stand at very different
stages of this general process, we find three different
kinds of phonetic influence on the pronunciation of
Putonghua.

1. Pre-nasal vowels are nasalized, and the final nasal consonant is dropped. Thus yu yan, 'language', is not [yü yɛn] but [yü yɛ̃]; san, 'three', is not [san] but [sã]. In Henan and Shaanxi provinces, we found that this pronunciation was quite general, we heard very few speakers observing the Peking standard pronunciation. The modified pronunciation of Putonghua that was cited above in Section 1, is not untypical. Many northern dialects have extreme nasalization through many segments. We would frequently be greeted by vice-chairmen of Revolutionary Committees with the word péngyoumen, pronounced [pʌ̃youmĩ].

2. When we visited Yenan, we found that the local pronunciation of this place name was not [jɛ́nãn] but [jæ:ŋ], where the medial nasal is elided altogether, and the final nasal realized as a velar. For a number of dialects, both nasal finals fall together as /ŋ/, as in many Spanish dialects of the Caribbean, and this appears of course in pronunciations of Putonghua as well.

3. The final stage in the reduction of final nasals is the loss of the nasalization altogether. This is a recognized feature of many dialects, and can lead to a great deal of homonymy. In Sian this loss of nasalization is quite common. Sān lóu, 'third floor', is [sā lóu].

(R): A second major variable in Putonghua is the maintenance of the retroflex series as distinct from the dentals or alveolars. The Peking standard has the following three series of affricates and fricatives:

|  | pinyin | dental or alveolar | pinyin | retroflex | pinyin | alveolo-palatal |
|---|---|---|---|---|---|---|
| aspirated affricates | c | $ts^h$ | ch | $tṣ^h$ | q | $tɕ^h$ |
| unaspirated affricates | z | ts | zh | tṣ | j | tɕ |
| fricatives | s | s | sh | ṣ | x | ɕ |

In most of the areas that we visited outside of Peking, we heard no distinction between the first two series or else great variability; again, only a small number of speakers made the distinctions. Thus we would typically hear

Zhongguo, 'China' as [tsɑŋgwɔ] rather than [tʂɑŋgwɔ], shuo,
'speak', as [swɔ], and so on.  This merger produces a vast
amount of homonymy, and can cause real confusion.

Despite the fact that this major distinction is well
recognized as a problem for teachers of Putonghua, and
discussed in every classroom, it seems that the effective
standard of pronunciation must tolerate the merger.  We
rarely heard a speaker of Wu or southeastern dialects who
had mastered the distinction entirely, which involves dividing three major word classes into two sets, morpheme
by morpheme.  In Canton, we found that the problem was in-
formally recognized as beyond immediate solution; though
some effort was made to teach the distinction, there were
many more serious difficulties to overcome in teaching
Putonghua.

(N-L):  Initial /n/ and /l/ have merged for a number
of dialects.  In some instances the interference is not
due to a complete merger but to a sporadic change.  One
museum guide in Sian seemed to have excellent Putonghua,
with Peking-style pronunciation.  But one word stood out
as odd: instead of nóng-yè, 'agriculture', she regularly
said lóng-yè.  When she was asked about this, she said,
"Oh yes, I can never remember which one that is."  Another
common word which gave her trouble was dà lù, 'highway',
which might have been dà nù as far as she was concerned.
This young woman had gone to Peking University, and learned
Putonghua quite well, but the /n/∿/l/ problem still remained.

(R-L):  Other dialects merge initial /r/ and /l/.
Thus our staff member frequently said luguo instead of
ruguo for 'if', though he used both forms.

We noted many other variables concerning the quality
of nuclei in Putonghua, but none of these seemed to be
major concerns of those trying to teach the standard pronunciation.  There is an enormous amount of variation in
the height of the nucleus in the /ou/ diphthong, so that
we heard liù 'six' forms ranging from [liù] to [liɜu].
Similarly, we noted a great deal of monophthongization of
/ai/ and /au/, so that we heard kāi mén 'open door' frequently as [khɛ̄mə́n], and dao 'arrive' is often [tɔ̀].  But
if these are sociolinguistic variables, they are indicators

that are well below the level of conscious reaction.
   There are also many perturbations of the tone system
due to the conflict between the Putonghua system and the
local dialects.  As noted above, much of the effort of
the Shanghai dialect studies has gone into charting such
relations.  In various places in China, one often hears
Putonghua spoken with tones that are strikingly different
from the standard.  For example, as our bus arrived at
the guest house in Linxian, one of our escorts said, dǎo
le, 'we have arrived' with low rising tone instead of the
Putonghua high falling tone dào le.

## 4.3  Sociolinguistic factors

   In the discussion above, we indicated that very few
speakers in areas outside of Peking had mastered the details of the standard pronunciation of Putonghua.  This
was true in Linxian, Zhengzhou, Yenan, Sian, Shanghai,
Suzhou, Hangzhou, and Canton.  Some very striking social
patterns emerged when we considered which speakers had
actually used the Peking phonetics.

   (1)   Some university professors

   (2)   Some female high school teachers of Chinese,
         trained in Peking

   (3)   Female guides as at museums and exhibition halls.

Since it has been shown in a number of societies, including
the United States, that women are more sensitive to prestige standard in language than men, it was interesting to
discover that the same pattern exists in China.  The pre-
cision of articulation of many of these female speakers
was quite striking, and was associated with a very erect
posture, compressed lips, and a bright, serious and ear-
nest expression.  It is worth noting that almost all
announcers in China are women, who use a similar clipped
and forcefully articulated style over the radio, and at
stage performances; this style is imitated by little
girls who announce school plays and dances.
   The greatest contrast with this standard pronunciation
is heard from younger men who were leading members of Revolutionary Committees in charge of educational institutions, in regard to the variables discussed above and many
others.

## 5.  Progress Towards Achieving Linguistic Goals

In the first three sections we outlined the goals of
modern Chinese society in regard to language; and in the
fourth section we reported some observations about the
linguistic situation today.  Here we will attempt to give
a brief assessment of the progress that Chinese society
has made towards achieving those goals, bearing in mind
that our observations were quite brief and our understanding of the whole situation necessarily limited.  For the
most part we will be reporting assessments that are reinforced by opinions expressed by our Chinese hosts themselves.

## 5.1  The Standardization of Putonghua

The issue of popularizing Putonghua is the concern of
the next chapter.  Here we would ask whether the form that
Putonghua is beginning to assume corresponds with the
goals that were set forth in the official Chinese position.
It seems clear that Putonghua is functioning effectively as a medium of wider communication in China.  The longer
range problem is whether this medium will tend to develop
regional varieties of its own, as more and more speakers
of various substrata acquire it as their native vernacular.
There is good reason to think that widespread lexical
borrowing into Putonghua will take place if local dialects
give way.  Since the Chinese system is to operate by
persuasion rather than prescription, it will be interesting
to see what measures will be taken to control regionaliza-
tion of the standard.
As far as the phonological system is concerned, a good
guess would be that the retroflex-dental distinction will
not be maintained in the emerging common language.  The
general principle here is that mergers expand at the ex-
pense of distinctions, and it would take a major national
effort to reverse this principle in China.  There is no
reason to think that the effort will be worth the gain,
since Chinese is already developing polysyllabic words
which offset the widespread homonymy that now exists.  No
doubt northern speakers will continue to make the distinction in their Putonghua, but when they use the Putonghua
to communicate with speakers of other dialects--the primary

purpose of the common language--they must expect that the
other speakers will not be able to use this distinction
to separate word classes.

Many individuals have undertaken to achieve standard
pronunciation of their Putonghua as a serious political
goal. This is certainly true of many teachers that we
met; such intensive mobilization will be necessary if the
common language is to maintain its unity. On the other
hand, it would seem that some variables will be maintained
to signal important social messages. As a first guess,
it seems that in many areas extreme nasalization of vowels
and loss of final nasals functions as a distinguishing
mark of local identity and alignment with the style of
workers and peasants.

This does not mean that China is showing a class stratification of language parallel to the patterns described
in New York, Detroit, Paris or Norwich. The covert prestige of working-class style in New York is overt prestige
here, and there seems to be no pressure on speakers to
emulate the patterns of intellectuals or officials in
order to get ahead in society. One would have to know
this revolutionary society much better in order to speak
more concretely about sources of prestige. However, it
is clear that the official status of Peking pronunciation
is competing with other sources of status. Leading members
of revolutionary committees tell us that they really spoke
dialect rather than Putonghua, referring to the heavy local
influence on their Putonghua. These statements are made
without shame or embarrassment, and the sparkle of local
pride below the surface is not hard to detect. This
feeling may be supported by the observation that many
national leaders are from the South and speak Putonghua
with a noticeable accent.

There are some social situations in which the use of
local dialects is already seen as quite inappropriate.
When members of our delegation asked an exhibition guide
in Linxian to speak her local dialect as she lectured to
us, she did so, but with a great deal of joking and nervous
laughter. There is a tendency for audiences to laugh when
someone quotes dialect forms outside of context. But this
does not mean that the local dialect is the subject of
ridicule. At Fudan University, we made a point of asking
about the reason for this: are speakers of local dialect

considered to be ignorant or comical? The vice-chairman
of the Revolutionary Committee intervened, saying that
most of those present spoke dialect better than Putonghua:
they themselves were the dialect speakers we were talking
about.

## 5.2  The Use of Putonghua

One of the major aims of the Chinese revolution is to
break down the barriers between schools and the world of
everyday working people, changing a system which centered
about the teacher, the classroom and the text, and ending
the divorce from workers, from politics, and from reality.
To a large extent, this has been achieved by bringing
students into contact with the farmers and workers physically and ideologically.  The question is whether or not
the emerging common language, as it is used in the classroom, actually reflects the everyday language of workers
and peasants.

The most common linguistic models that are held up to
Chinese students to emulate are the writings of Chairman
Mao and of Lu Hsun.  Even an outsider to the Chinese language can easily absorb some of the force of direct expression and the colloquial vigor of their styles.  At
Yenan, we heard many stories about Chairman Mao, with long
quotations from the way he expressed himself in a crisis;
many of his reported comments brought instant laughter
from those in the audience who understood Chinese.  The
same reaction could be observed at many of our briefing
sessions with leading members of revolutionary committees.
It was natural for them to use expressions drawn from
everyday life which were not typical of everyday language.

At the same time, it would be premature to think that
the issue which was raised in Chairman Mao's "Oppose Stereotyped Party Writing" is resolved.

At a Peking high school, we asked a teacher of Chinese
how students had learned from the rich and vigorous language of the peasants when they went to the countryside
as part of the Open Door Way policy.  Among the expressions
he quoted were a number of phrases modeled on folk rhymes:

    tiān dà hàn              'the nature has a serious drought'
    rén dà gàn               'the people work the hardest'
    dì li liǎng dùn fàn      'in the field we eat two meals'
    bái tiān yè li lián zhōu zhuàn
                             'day and night we work contin-
                                 uously'

Almost in every briefing during our visit, we noticed the
use of rhymes in describing struggles against nature and
against the ideology of the past.

When we heard that students at a Shanghai school had
written down the life experiences of working men, we asked
to read one of the examples. It was a very good composition, by any school standards; but it did not seem to transmit any of the personal experience of the man he was writing about. We are judging by comparison with narratives
of personal experience gathered in other sociolinguistic
studies: it may very well be that ordinary Chinese people
express their deepest thoughts and experiences in standard
political formulations. But if that is true, there is no
reason for students to go to them to learn that language:
they might have learned it from the newspaper.

To transmit the language of everyday life to the school-
room is a challenging task. If the Chinese educators and
linguists have not yet achieved this, it is not because
they do not take their goals seriously. The problem is
a hard one, and the traditional forces operating in the
other direction are strong.

Another aspect of the use of language in the classroom
is the Chinese policy of encouraging free discussion.
In the first ten classrooms we visited, we saw many interesting innovations, and some striking achievements,
but we did not see any discussion. No student asked any
questions and all the interaction was initiated by the
teacher.

In one third grade, students sat bolt upright, with
their hands neatly folded in front of them. When someone wanted to answer, he pivoted his forearm into vertical position, holding his elbow firmly in place.

At Shaanxi Normal College, on the other hand, we had a
good discussion with students in an English class, but

such discussions are quite formal.  The subject was set by
the teacher, who called on the first two speakers, and he
moderated the rest of the session like a town meeting.

In the general discussion, we asked about this problem,
and we were frankly told that it is not easy to overcome
the long tradition of respect for the teacher.  It was
said that in the old days five out of every ten questions
were not answered at all, and students learned not to ask
questions out of fear of embarrassing the teacher who might
not know the answer.  Chinese educators are trying to
change this situation, but they have a long way to go.  It
was also pointed out to us that a great deal of learning
takes place in informal study groups, where students help
each other and engage in vigorous discussion.  Since opportunities to observe these groups are rare, we were
left with our impressions of the formal classroom setting.

However, we were fortunate enough to observe a third
grade class at Shanghai's Cao Yang 1st Primary School.
For almost an hour, we saw three-quarters of the students
on their feet, leaning out of their chairs, and waving
their hands, anxious to be recognized.  They had just
been down to the docks to look at the big ships that the
Chinese people had built, and everyone had something to
say.  The teacher was firm and rather sharp, but nothing
she said dampened their desire to speak up.  She called
on one student:  "Shèn."  He stood up, saying: "You made
a mistake.  My name isn't Shèn.  In Putonghua, it's Shěn."
The teacher accepted this in stride.  Another student got
up to say that China had built boats that sail all the
way across the world.  A girl stood up to say: "You're
wrong.  You should say, 'Because of the great Cultural
Revolution, China was able to build boats that would sail
across the world.'"  A third student jumped up and said
to her: "You're wrong to criticize him like that.  Why
do you only point out what he said that was wrong?  First
you should say what's good about him and then say what's
bad."

In this third grade class, we saw proof that the goals
of the Chinese educational revolution could be achieved.
However, the problem is not being attacked on a centralized basis.  Each area seems to be proceeding on its own
initiative, making different degrees of progress towards
the general goal.

## 3. LANGUAGE REFORM

### Introduction

The language reform movement in China is without parallel in the magnitude of the problems and number of people
affected, in the systematic nature of its planning and implementation, and in the degree of involvement of the masses.
The comparative study of language planning processes which
has been developing recently has, however, paid relatively little attention to China. Even the recent American
studies of Chinese language planning have had little to
report on events since 1964. In this chapter we offer information on the whole language reform movement for those
interested in the study of language planning processes,
and we provide material on developments since 1964 which
may be of special value to those interested in Chinese
studies.

The language reform movement has three aspects (1) the
simplification of characters, that is, reduction in the
number of strokes in Chinese characters and elimination
of variants and unnecessary characters; (2) the popularization of the common speech, Putonghua; and (3) the creation and popularization of a national phonetic alphabet.
After a historical introduction, and an account of the
Committee on Language Reform, which is the principal language planning agency, we will discuss each of these aspects in turn.

On Thursday afternoon October 24, the members of the
Delegation met in Peking with four representatives of the
Chinese Committee on Language Reform (Wenzi Gaige
Weiyuanhui) to discuss the current status of language re-
form in China. The Committee representatives present were
Ye Lai-shi, Responsible Person of the Committee, Chen
Nai-hua, Cao Cheng-fang, and Sun Jian. The Chinese spoke
for about two hours on the history and current status of

language reform activities, and after this the Delegation
asked a number of questions, to which Mr. Ye replied in
detail, in a frank, open and friendly manner.

The American Delegation, especially those who spoke
Chinese and had had considerable experience with Chinese
language questions, also had the opportunity to ask opinions
of others and observe people's actual use of language during their visit to other institutions and in their travels
about the country.  This chapter summarizes the new information available together with the opinions of the Delegation on some of the issues raised.

1.  History

Public planning of language questions in China goes
back at least as far as 213 B.C. with the unification of
characters undertaken by Li Si as part of Chin Shi
Huang Di's unification of China.  Li Si published an official list of over 3000 characters which eliminated many
variant forms of characters.  He apparently also provided
uniform terminology and forms of discourse for official
correspondence and public documents.  Succeeding gener-
ations, however, kept adding to the number of characters,
the complexity of individual characters, and the variant
form of characters.  On the other hand, many users of the
language have also simplified the characters in their handwriting; in the present ideology this is seen as a contri-
bution of the masses in opposition to the elitism of the
scholars.

The written language has been seen as a unifying factor
throughout the history.  In the spread of a common spoken
language the dialect of Peking has had a natural pre-
eminence, at least since the location of the capital in
Peking in the fourteenth century.  Side by side with the
literary language the spoken vernacular was used in certain
kinds of literature; in the early days of the republic a
campaign spearheaded by the May 4th movement in 1919 advocated the use of the modern spoken language as the sole
basis for written Chinese.

Through the history of the Chinese language the extent
to which characters are phoneticized, that is, give an indication of pronunciation as opposed to meaning, has varied
greatly.  Since the earliest characters were almost purely ideographic and most characters in use today (although

not some of the commonest) have a phonetic component, it
is possible to maintain that in general the trend of
Chinese writing has been toward increased phonetization.
This view is now presented as a partial justification for
transforming the Chinese writing system into a phonetic
alphabet; the other justification offered is that almost
all other languages in the world have alphabetic writing
systems. Modern attempts at alphabetization began in the
nineteenth century and a number of schemes were supported
by various groups from 1911 to 1949.

Chairman Mao and the Chinese Communist Party went on
record very early in favor of language reform of all three
kinds: character simplification, popularization of Putonghua,
and the phonetic alphabet. In 1940 Chairman Mao said "The
written language must be reformed" and in 1951 he went further in adding it should take the direction of phonetization. Ten days after Liberation in 1949 an Association
for Language Reform was established which became in 1952
the Research Committee on Language Reform under government auspices. This was reorganized as the Committee on
Language Reform and placed directly under the State Council in 1954. Its task was to make the Chinese language
serve the workers and peasants and to further socialist
construction. In October 1955 it sponsored a National
Conference on the Reform of the Chinese Written Language,
which was followed in the same month by a Conference on
the Standardization of Modern Chinese (Xiandai hanyu
guifanhua wenti xueshu huiyi). The first conference,
basing its action on a widely circulated draft plan of
character simplification and six alternative alphabets
presented by the Committee, issued its recommendations on
language reform: an amended form of the draft plan for
simplification and a Latin alphabet orthography, pinyin.
The simplification plan was adopted by the State Council
in January 1956, and the Latinization plan was dissemina-
ted to local authorities throughout the country by the
Committee itself in February 1956. The Standardization
Conference defined and endorsed Putonghua.

2. Organization of the Committee on Language Reform

At present the Committee consists of over twenty members,
with an office staff of over thirty. It continues to have
the same membership as in the past, but some consideration

is being given to possible broadening of committee membership because of aging members and deaths. The Committee
meets only rarely, for discussion of an important problem or proposed scheme.

The staff consists of four main groups who deal with:

(1) The collection of simplified characters in use
by the masses or suggested by them, standardization of
these, and the preparation of draft lists of simplified
characters for consideration by the Committee.

(2) Activities for popularizing both Putonghua and
the use of pinyin.

(3) Research in specialized or new uses of pinyin,
for example, in telegraphic communication.

(4) Propaganda activities such as the organization
of people to write articles on language reform for newspapers and magazines.

The Committee maintains close connections with educational institutions. It works on some theoretical problems with the cooperation of universities and scientific
institutions, and some specialists from universities are
members of the Committee. Staff members often travel to
different parts of the country to conduct investigations;
much of the work sponsored by the Committee or reflecting
the aims of the Committee is also carried out by local organizations.

In response to a question about similar committees or
organizations elsewhere, the Committee on Language Reform
of Xinjiang was mentioned as being very active in the popularization of the new orthographies for Uighur and Kazakh.
In most cities, however, the work is usually carried out
by bureaus of education.

Other countries carry out their language planning activities by different sorts of language planning agencies.
In some instances the principal agency is an autonomous,
prestigious academy consisting of a limited number of outstanding individuals selected for life. Typically, such
academies publish long-range projects such as exhaustive
historical dictionaries, do relatively little in the

implementation of their language planning decisions, and
serve social functions other than language planning (e.g.,
the Hebrew Language Academy in Israel). In other instances the principal language planning agency is a well-
staffed institute which carries on extensive implementation
activities in publishing, teacher training, etc. and calls
on experts to meet with the staff for language planning
decisions (e.g., the Diwan Bahasa Pustaka in Malaysia).
China has opted for a high-level committee which promul-
gates decisions at rare intervals and makes use of a
staff which does research required for its decisions,
initiates or supports implementation activities of various
kinds, and carries out appropriate promotional and propaganda efforts. The committee receives its official back-
ing, when needed, from the highest government level, the
State Council.

Two features of the Chinese pattern are of particular
interest: the *ad hoc* nature of the main language planning
agency and the exclusion of lexicography and technical
vocabulary development from its responsibilities.

The Committee on Language Reform is not an autonomous
permanent institution like an academy or institute, but
an appointed committee whose membership has been constant
for twenty years and which has no functions apart from
language planning activities.

In many countries the development of technical vocabulary is regarded as a major task of language planning and
one of the most prominent activities of the chief language
planning agency. In China this task is almost completely
separated from the Committee on Language Reform. The Committee does have some lexical concerns, but these are either
with selecting the standard one of a set of competing
synonyms or with assuring the enrichment of the lexicon
with particularly apt or vivid words and expressions from
the workers, peasants and soldiers. The creation and standardization of technical terms is handled elsewhere. The
Delegation did not pursue this point, and no reference was
made to the continued existence or current activities of
the Terminology Section of the Academy of Sciences, which
has done some of this work in the past. Inquiries made in
factories and workshops about sources of new terminology
brought replies suggesting on the one hand that new terminology is kept to a minimum and integrated with practice,
and on the other hand that units within appropriate

ministries in Peking provide necessary vocabulary for new
machines, etc. and disseminate it throughout the country.
The most recent technical dictionary seen on the visit
was an extensive English-Japanese-Chinese dictionary of
radio and electronic terminology arranged for the use of
Chinese reading technical material in English or Japanese.
The Chinese equivalents in it were often definitional or
descriptive rather than corresponding technical terms.
The language planning area of lexical elaboration and the
creation of new expressions and forms of discourse needs
further systematic study by language planning specialists
and by scholars of Chinese linguistics.

## 3.  Character Simplification (<u>hanzi jianhua</u>)

Most of the language reform efforts in China up to
1949 were concerned with schemes for alphabetization,
but after the establishment of the People's Republic in
1949 the top priority in language reform went to character simplification.  This aspect of language reform has
been actively followed up to the present; we were told
that the Committee on Language Reform has a new list of simplified characters about to be published.

A list of commonly used simplified characters was published as early as 1950.  After extensive research and discussion the Committee on Language Reform together with the
Ministry of Education published an extensive draft of proposed simplified characters.  This draft list was distributed in 300,000 copies for experimentation and discussion.
On January 28, 1956 the State Council promulgated a list
of 544 characters, of which twenty-nine were to be abolished and 515 simplified in form.  Comparison of these
simplified characters with their original forms shows an
average reduction from sixteen strokes to eight strokes
per character.  In 1964 the Committee published a list of
over two thousand simplified characters, many of them re-
sulting from the use of simplified components which appear
in more than one character.  In that same year the Department of Culture and the Committee published a list of over
6000 standard characters for the use of printing houses.
The traditional 214 "radicals," the components by which
many dictionaries are arranged, were reduced to 189.

Since 1964 the Committee on Language Reform has been
collecting characters simplified by the masses.  In 1973

it published the <u>Hanzi Zhengzi Xiao Zihui</u> (<u>Chugao</u>), a
small dictionary of Chinese characters in which newly simplified characters are included. The Committee is making
systematic studies of all these simplified characters,
and a draft list of them will be submitted to the central
government for approval. The approved draft list will
again be distributed to the masses for discussion and
comments. The Committee will then prepare a definitive
list for official approval. Mr. Ye told us that a list
of about 100 simplified characters would be formally promulgated sometime in 1975.

Nowadays virtually all new publications are printed in
simplified characters. We were told that the original characters are used only in some rare cases, such as the printing
of ancient texts for historical studies of the writing system. Photographic reproductions of earlier writings in complicated characters which have value in calligraphic arts also exist.

On the streets, generally speaking, shop signs are in simplified characters, although a few signs in special calligraphic styles may retain complicated characters. For example, in <u>Zhōngguó Rénmín Yínháng</u> 'Chinese People's Bank' the
characters <u>guó</u> and <u>yín</u> are not simplified. Quotations of
Chairman Mao if in his handwriting may contain complicated
characters.

Simplified characters are taught in schools; we were
told that some pupils easily learned to read the complicated characters at home from the books printed earlier.
Adults, especially older people, may sometimes write their
own names in complicated characters.

During the visit we saw quite a few newly simplified
characters not yet officially approved. They appeared,
for example, in mimeographed performance programs and in
the slogans on walls. For example, the slogan "In agriculture learn from Dazhai" appeared in two ways:

农 业 学 大 寨

农 业 学 大 寀

The character 寀 is a newly simplified character. The
component 在 zài is not homophonous with <u>zhai</u>, but rhymes
with it. The following are some other newly simplified
characters:

| original | simplified | pronunciation | meaning |
|----------|------------|---------------|---------|
| 餐 | 歺 | cān | 'meal' |
| 酒 | 氿 | jiǔ | 'wine' |
| 漆 | 汢 | qī | 'paint' |
| 稻 | 秒 | dào | 'rice crops' |
| 副 | 付 | fù | 'deputy' |
| 賽 | 宷 | sài | 'to compete' |

There seems to be a common direction of simplification of characters having many strokes. The direction is to make these characters analyzable into components which are words in their own right or can be pronounced separately. For example, the character 宰 now has a top-bottom composition. The top is the <u>bǎo gài tóu</u> 'the cover radical' and the bottom is the word <u>zài</u> 'to be at'. The formation of such a tendency of simplification may have to do with how characters are taught at schools. From the first grade on students learn to analyze characters into components (see Chapter 4). Naturally, characters with sayable components are easier to analyze and remember. Usually simpler characters are used for the phonetic components.

## 4. Popularization of Putonghua (<u>tuiguang putonghua</u>)

Apart from the six percent of the population who speak minority languages such as Mongolian or Tibetan, the Chinese people all speak what may be regarded as the same language, sometimes called Han to distinguish it from the non-Han minority languages which also may be called Chinese in the broader sense. Some of the local varieties of Han differ greatly from one another and some are to a large degree mutually unintelligible. There are at least eight major dialect groups which differ sufficiently to be called separate languages if it were not for the attitudes of the speakers and the tradition of a single written language. The largest is the North Chinese dialect group which includes at least seventy percent of the Han speakers; the others are Wu, Xiang, Gan, Hakka, Northern Min, Southern

Min, and Cantonese, each spoken by millions of people.
Although there is a fundamental unity of vocabulary and
grammar, these dialects differ strikingly in such basic
features as the pronoun systems. Their phonologies show
great differences in such features as tone systems and
permitted final consonants. (Min = Fukienese--cf. p. 11)

For over 500 years written Chinese has tended to be
based to some extent on the kind of North Chinese spoken
in Peking. Mandarin Chinese or guanhua 'official language,'
which long served as a lingua franca in China was based on
an earlier variety of Peking speech. Thus the 1955/56
decision to promote essentially Peking Chinese as the common language recognized and reinforced an existing trend.

The State Council asked all the schools of the nation
to use Putonghua as the medium of instruction beginning
in autumn 1956, thus changing the dominant pattern of
using the local dialect as the medium. During the period
1956-60 the Committee on Language Reform cooperated with
other agencies in mounting ten workshops on the phonetics
of Putonghua, for a total of 2000 persons trained for
popularization of Putonghua. Between 1958 and 1964 four
conferences were held to exchange experience in the popularization. Teachers gained experience, school students
gave demonstrations, and more and more people came to believe in the cause of popularizing Putonghua.

In 1958 three important events took place: Premier Chou
En-lai announced that the popularization of Putonghua was
an important political task, the People's Congress approved
the use of pinyin as a tool for the spread of Putonghua,
and Chairman Mao declared that all cadres (party and administrative workers) must.learn to speak Putonghua.

The county of Datian in Fujian province was cited as an
example of the progress achieved. It has three major and
over ten minor dialects— "people separated by a blade of
grass could not understand each other." A cadre from the
North needed three to seven interpreters to make a speech.
Party leaders took an active role in promoting Putonghua,
concentrating on schools, evening schools, and public
gathering places; and recently in the movement to criticize
Lin Piao and Confucius there was further advance in the
popularization of Putonghua. In a recent radio report a
county official addressed 120,000 people without need of
an interpreter.

The basic policy for spreading Putonghua consists of

three principles, referred to as the "twelve-character principles": (1) to encourage people to speak Putonghua on more occasions, (2) to select particular places and social groups for promotion and (3) to go gradually, "step-by-step." For example, people are encouraged to use Putonghua with newcomers from other provinces, and on formal occasions. Experiments are made in selecting sites and populations: schools, young people generally, post offices and telegraph offices. For example, Shanghai, one of the areas where the Putonghua promotion has been most successful, selected five types of people: shop attendants, members of hotel staffs, streetcar and bus conductors, railroad conductors, broadcasters. As part of the principle of gradual change it is recognized that not everyone needs to speak Putonghua exactly as Peking people do.

The policy with regard to local dialects is that they also are useful and Putonghua is to be taught in addition to the local dialect. Cadres should learn to use the dialect of the area in which they work. The policy in minority language areas is different. In such places Putonghua is to be taught only in response to the wishes of the local population to acquire it; and when Han-speaking people go to work in minority areas they are to learn the local language. In general it is recognized that the popularization of a common language in such a large and complex country as China is a difficult task, which requires continuous effort over a long period of time.

Two special points are worth noting for any attempt at comparison with similar efforts in other countries or for estimating the probable outcome in China: regional differences in implementation and value orientation toward dialects. Although we saw no evidence whatever of resistance to the Putonghua policy, it was clear that the success differs in different areas and the degree of commitment also differs. Canton and Shanghai contrasted in that the school students in Shanghai seemed much more enthusiastic about promoting Putonghua among the people, although in both places the children were able to use it effectively in school and in conversing with outsiders. And in both places they were also able to use the local dialect when appropriate.

Nowhere did people seem to regard the local dialect as inferior or shameful. On some occasions use of the dialect is felt to be inappropriate, but the preference for

Putonghua seems to be on the grounds of national unity or
need for communication rather than superiority or correctness.  Moreover, great leeway is allowed on certain features
of pronunciation, such as sibilants and affricates (see
Chapter 2.4).  Even though there may be good-natured poking
of fun at local accents in Putonghua, there seems to be no
stigma attached to such pronunciations.  The factors accoun-
ting for this set of attitudes are doubtless complex, but
we may note that many of the national leaders do not come
from North Chinese regions and pronounce Putonghua with
regional accents.

## 5.  Phonetic Alphabet (pinyin)

Before the creation of the present pinyin alphabetic
writing in 1956/58, three other schemes had received prominent attention.  The National Phonetic Alphabet, which
emerged from a conference in 1913 in Peking on unification
of pronunciation, used symbols based on Chinese characters.
The romanization ("Gwoyeu Romatzyh") constructed by Y. R.
Chao and four other scholars in 1925-26, used roman letters
and indicated the tones by the spelling in a fairly complicated system.  "Latinhua" 'Latinization' or "Xinwenzi"
'new writing,' also used roman letters but indicated tones
by diacritics and only when necessary to resolve an ambi-
guity; it was adopted by a conference in Haishenwei
(Vladisvostok) in 1913 for Chinese in the U.S.S.R.  The
last was promoted intensively in the Soviet Union from
1931-37 and to some extent in China, especially 1940-43
in liberated areas.

Most of the argumentation and policy shifts in all these
schemes including pinyin have revolved around three questions of structure and three questions of use.  The questions about structure are the following: Should the script
be "national" in nature, resembling traditional Chinese
writing, or should it adopt a "foreign" alphabet, and if
the latter, which one?  How should the tones be represented in it?  Should it be monosyllabic or by words, and if
the latter, how?

Chairman Mao's words of 1951: "Our written language
must be reformed; it should take the direction of phonetization common to all the languages of the world" are
quoted as the guideline for the pinyin policy.  Originally, however, he added "it must be national in form."  This

matter has recurred from time to time.  The present policy
has dropped any idea of an alphabet derived from Chinese
characters and explicitly rejects the Cyrillic alphabet.
The Committee on Language Reform sees the roman pinyin as
the final solution, leaving open for change— apart from
possible minor readjustments— only the questions of tone
and word division, which are felt to need further consideration.  It may be noted here that the four tone diacritics
are widely used in teaching even without pinyin.  For
example, they are sometimes written above Chinese characters in teaching pronunciation to dialect speakers and
foreigners; teachers of deaf mutes use gestures iconic to
them in drilling on tones.  On the other hand, word division usage varies considerably.  For example, some public
signs have space between syllables, some have space roughly
at word boundaries, and some run the text together without
spaces.

The three questions about use are as follows: Should the
alphabet also be used to represent Han dialects and non-Han
minority languages?  Should popularization of Putonghua be
completed before the use of pinyin is substantially increased?  Should pinyin ultimately replace the Chinese
characters altogether?

The principal uses of pinyin at present are to facilitate the learning of Chinese characters, and to facilitate
the speed of Putonghua popularization, primarily for Chinese-
speakers but also for minorities and foreigners (see Chapter 4.1).  It is also used in sending telegrams in the rail-
way administration in North China and as an alphabetic or-
dering of dictionaries and indices.  There seems to be no
policy of using pinyin for writing local dialects, but the
policy of using pinyin for minority languages is continuing
and even becoming stronger.  Ten orthographies based on
pinyin have been created for previously unwritten minority
languages: Zhuang, Miao, Yi, Dong, Buyi, Li, Hani, Lisu,
Wa, Naxi.  Four nationalities have replaced their traditional writing system by one based on pinyin: Uighur,
Jingpo, Kazakh, and Lahu.  For two of these, Uighur and
Kazakh, campaigns for the promotion of the new script are
in progress.

The five principles followed in creating and reforming
orthographies are these:

(1)  All alphabets should be romanized.

(2)  If a phoneme is similar to a Han phoneme the pinyin symbol should be used.

(3)  If there is no Han counterpart a new diacritic or special letter should be created.

(4)  The orthography of related languages should be consistent.

(5)  Loanwords from Han Chinese should be spelled as they are in the Chinese pinyin.

On the relative timing of the spread of Putonghua and pinyin, some have held the view that widespread use of pinyin could not be successful unless people had already acquired Putonghua; present policy seems to be that while the use of pinyin should only be extended gradually, it will not be necessary to wait until the full spread of Putonghua for great expansion of pinyin.

Finally, the question of ultimate replacement of characters remains unclear.  The spokesman for the Committee on Language Reform noted that many departments use pinyin in textbooks and that Chinese language lessons in the magazine China Reconstructs and in instructional material accompanying brochures use pinyin.  Also, in addition to past actions such as the creation of a pinyin-based finger-spelling for the deaf, pinyin braille for the blind and code for telegraphy, new uses are evident in the names of products, flag signals, indices, and foreign place names. He also commented that a recent Central Broadcasting Station program popularizing pinyin was welcomed by workers, peasants, and teachers and was rebroadcast in many places.

When we asked why pinyin is not used for proper names in foreign language publications printed in China, Mr. Ye told us that beginning in 1975 all such publications will use the pinyin romanization for place names.  He also mentioned the recently published map of China in pinyin and said that a list of Chinese place names in pinyin had already been sent to the United Nations for a worldwide compilation of place names.

It is clear that in many instances the party and the government have not pushed campaigns where they would be possible.  For example, the use of pinyin in telegraphy has not been strongly promoted.  It is possible that the caution results from unresolved differences of opinion in the leadership; but we have the impression that the ultimate

goal is full shift to alphabetization, though the policy
is one of extreme gradualness.  As indicated in Section 3,
however, the popularization of Putonghua is vigorously
promoted, and has been highly successful.  Language reform
accordingly varies in the emphasis placed on the three aspects cited in the introduction to this chapter, as on the
success of their implementation.

# 4. THE TEACHING OF CHINESE


## 1. Primary and Middle Schools

Children begin their introduction to the written language of Putonghua when they enter primary school, typically at seven. Most have attended nursery school and
kindergarten previously. Pinyin is the first writing
system studied.

The pinyin system is introduced beginning with the
names of the consonants, e.g., [puo tə kə]. Then vowels
are introduced, followed by the nasal finals, and subsequently the diphthongs. Syllables are learned and analyzed as consisting of two parts, the initial, and the
final--an analysis which reflects a long history of Chinese
linguistic tradition. For example, a student pronouncing
the syllable hóng, will say something like [xə̄], [ɔ̄ŋ],
[xɔ́ŋ], the h being a voiceless velar fricative.

The time allotted for learning pinyin varies according
to the locality. In areas with strong interference from
another dialect, more time is needed. The basic time
allotments in Mandarin-speaking areas are four or five
weeks of study. In Canton, which may be representative
of non-Mandarin areas, six weeks are generally allotted
for the initial presentation of pinyin.

By the end of the second year of school, students will
be able to spell and pronounce syllables written in pinyin,
and to utilize pinyin in learning new words and correcting
local accents. By the time students are in the third grade,
they will be able to use pinyin to look up words in a dictionary and to read simple texts in pinyin. Beyond the
fourth grade level, students will be able to read texts
written in pinyin without difficulty and to transcribe
easily.

By the time students enter middle school, it is assumed

that they have mastered pinyin; it is no longer taught
but it is generally used.

Chinese characters are introduced after the initial
period of presentation of pinyin. When introduced, each
character is also given in pinyin. The student is taught
to describe the structure of the characters and their component parts. Basic strokes are identified by name, for
example, nà for a downward, right-slanting stroke, héng
for a horizontal stroke written from left to right. The
characters for the numbers from one to ten are utilized
in teaching the basic strokes, for they embody most of
the stroke types used in writing Chinese. In addition,
the students are taught popular names for frequent characters or parts of characters, usually radicals of the currently accepted 189 radical system. Frequent descriptors
for the remaining parts of characters are also taught
early. When more complicated characters are encountered,
they are broken down into their simpler components, often
by using a common word as descriptor. For example, the
character for hong 'red' (红) is divided into left and
right portions, the left being the radical for 'silk'
jiǎo-sī-páng (纟), and the right the character for 'work'
gōng (工), as in gong-ren ( 工人 ) 'worker'. In this way
the student is able to describe a character by its pronunciation, using pinyin, and by its traditional form.

Control of pinyin and the basic characters is assumed
on completion of primary school. When a student finishes
primary school he is expected to know 2800-3000 characters.
If, however, in writing a composition he needs a word for
which he has not yet learned the character, he is encouraged to write the word in pinyin. Middle schools essentially reinforce control of the writing system, and concentrate on content in their Chinese classes.

The curriculum in Chinese covers both language and
literature, ancient as well as modern.

It was pointed out to us in all the primary and middle
schools that the major aim of Chinese language instruction
is to change the ideology of the students and raise their
socialist consciousness. This aim is reflected in the
reading materials and lesson plans. In the Peking #15
Middle School, for example, we were told that the writings
of the Legalists are now studied in language classes as
part of the movement to criticize Lin Piao and Confucius;
the writings of Confucius are also read so that the students

can criticize them.  In another middle school, as noted
more fully below, we heard an excellent presentation of
the "Tian Lun" section of the philosopher Xun-zi (Hsün Tzu);
see Chapter 4.4.  In her presentation the teacher discussed
the contrast in usage between the modern vernacular and
classical Chinese, as well as the current interpretation
of the text.

Poetry and other literature are also interpreted from
an ideological point of view.  In Middle School #15 a poem
was the basis of the lesson; its analysis was not directed at the literary meaning of the poem but rather at its
revolutionary implications.  At the Cao Yang 1st Primary
School in Shanghai we observed a Chinese lesson in which
the students were learning to read from a collection of
short stories.  The one being read that day, Happiness
by Lu Xun (Lu Hsun), told of a fifteen year old girl who
martyred herself for the revolution.  In general then the
texts, whether modern or classical, are used as a basis
for instructing students in socialist ideology.

As with many foreign countries, education in the PRC
is more centralized than in the USA.  The educational processes seem to be directed by revolutionary committees,
which are found in every province, municipality, and social
system, such as schools.  These committees ensure that
party policies are carried out.  They also attempt to co-
ordinate one facet of life with another, so that education
will be associated with agriculture, factory work, health
services, welfare and so on.

In all the schools we visited we were told of the
changes in teaching technique and classroom procedures
which have occurred since the Cultural Revolution and
during the on-going Education Revolution.  In the efforts
to combine theory and practice, the humanities are to view
"society as their factory."  From the first grade of primary school, students spend a certain amount of time in
socially productive activity, either in the countryside,
factory, or school-run factories.  In some of the communities we visited, the schools were closed because of the
harvest.  In other schools students were assigned to work
for a month or more in school-attached factories.  Some
were involved in the production of chemicals, some were
making vacuum tubes, some were making simple mechanical
devices.  These operations were part of factories which
had placed the equipment in the schools.

In addition, as part of the Open Door Way, students
are organized to visit workers at home and at work, and
to go to peasant communes.  As part of their language
training they would then write compositions on what they
learned from these visits.  They are instructed to use
the rich language of the people in these assignments.
At times they also return to read these compositions, as
noted earlier; grades are awarded on consultation between
workers, teachers, and students.  Grades are based on
mastery of language and on political content.

School systems in the PRC then are open systems, so
much so that it is difficult to know where the systems
end and the environments begin.  Their activities enable
students to be in touch with the realities of life.  Moreover, parent and even student advice is seriously sought
after and translated into decision-making roles.

Classroom teaching, however, is quite traditional.
Most of the classes we visited had approximately fifty
students seated in seven or eight rows of seven seats
with attached desks.  Typically, on the back walls of the
classroom there were pictures of Marx, Engels, Lenin, and
Stalin with a picture of Chairman Mao at the front.  On
other walls there were red posters with sayings of Chairman Mao in white characters.  Other posters listed the
characters being studied, and in some rooms there were
phonetic diagrams.  Discipline in the classroom was strict.
For the most part there was little spontaneous discussion.
Upon being questioned students raised their right hands
with the elbows bent and rested on the desk.  In Shanghai,
however, we noted less rigidity; enthusiastic hand waving
occurred.  One student in our discussion told us that
this new freedom resulted from the Cultural Revolution,
which included struggles against regimentation in the
classroom.

Teachers use a variety of techniques, from choral repetition to relatively formal lectures.  Flash cards, charts
and other visual aids are well-designed, simple, and show
pedagogically sensitive use of color.  Many were done by
hand or printed or reproduced at low cost.  These aids
were used skillfully by all of the teachers we observed.

The conduct of classroom activity, in short, involves
a variety of interactive styles, all within a narrow range
of teacher and text-centered traditional forms.  Moreover,
the traditional styles are becoming more relaxed.  We saw

one teacher receive a correction from a student in class.
But we also saw some obvious errors go unchallenged until
the teacher corrected them herself.  Teaching styles ranged
from the warmly supportive, affectionate interaction of enthusiastic teachers and students to chilly, over-disciplined
classes, both at the same level.  Yet the level of teaching
is generally high.  We heard lectures on literary topics
delivered to middle school students that were literate
and polished to a degree worthy of college teaching in
some of our best institutions.

## 2.  Colleges and Universities

The aims of Chinese language teaching on the college
level are similar to those reported above.  At Zhongshan
University in Canton we were told that the goal of the
Chinese language department is to study Chinese from the
viewpoint of Marxism-Leninism and also to impart a wide
range of knowledge to cultural workers who can aid in the
popularization of Putonghua.  The Shanghai Normal University aims to train Chinese language teachers for the middle
schools and teachers for the state farm run by the University.

The curricula of the Chinese language departments in
the schools we visited were similar but not identical.
In Zhongshan University the subjects taught are general
linguistics, ancient and modern Chinese, Chinese characters,
character reform, Chinese dialects and the history of the
Chinese language.  The aims of instruction in these courses
were contrasted with the aims of courses before the Cultural
Revolution.  At that time the study of modern Chinese emphasized phonetics and grammar; now in the effort to popularize Putonghua, teachers and students are seeking faster
results through more practice and less theory.

Before the Cultural Revolution the history of the
Chinese language was also poorly studied because the materials were never related to a practical modern context.
Today, in learning the history of the language, students
must not only be able to read the ancient literature, but
also to analyze its content from the Marxist-Leninist
viewpoint.  As a result the study of ancient Chinese is
closely linked with the movement to criticize Lin Piao
and Confucius.  As an example, students last year examined
critically the "Doctrine of the Mean," published two

millennia ago. They annotated this work chapter by chapter. Now with the help of the annotations, other students
can read the work meaningfully. Accordingly, all study
of Chinese, whether of the modern or ancient language and
literature, must be undertaken in such a way that it con-
tributes to the aims of proletarian politics.

As in the primary and middle schools, Chinese instruction in the universities is conducted by the Open Door
method. Both faculty and students spend at least one
month of the year doing physical labor and learning from
the workers and peasants. In accordance with this aim
students majoring in Chinese at Peking University have
been conducting dialect studies in Shaoshan as noted in
Chapter 2, Section 3.2. After determining the dialect
characteristics, the students apply their findings to im-
proving the techniques of introducing Putonghua. In this
way the students serve society while putting theory into
practice.

3. Chinese as a Foreign Language

Foreigners who do not speak or read Chinese well enough
to attend Chinese institutions study Chinese intensively
at the Peking Language Institute (Beijing Yuyan Xueyuan),
or other language institutes. They stay in these institutes
as boarders for approximately one year. The teachers we
observed were able and experienced, with some competence
in the native language of the student, and knowledge of
the contrasts between the phonological and grammatical
systems of the two languages.

A basic set of materials is used for all languages,
with appropriate glosses in the student's native language.
Major changes in these materials are now in process; a
tentative edition of the first volume of the English text
is completed. This text, published in September 1974, is
entitled Hanyu Keben, Modern Chinese Reader, the same
English title given an earlier work published in 1959.

At the time of our visit there were 340 students in
residence, from forty foreign countries. The staff of the
Institute expects enrollments to increase as more governments recognize the government of the People's Republic
and conclude cultural exchange agreements that will provide
for study in China.

There has been much discussion of the principles of

teaching Chinese as a foreign language. Since practice
is viewed as fundamental in the dialectical-materialist
conception of learning, it is held that students can only
master a language through practice. The teacher must fill
the role of organizing and guiding students in this practice, and of stimulating their interest. During each stage
of learning, the students must master the material--words,
phrases and sentences--through practice. For in accordance with Chairman Mao's view of knowledge, perceptual
knowledge leads to rational knowledge, that is, to generalizations and theoretical understanding. Especially
in the first year, elaborate theoretical explanations con-
fuse rather than enlighten students.

On the other hand, the role of theory cannot be denied;
practice without theory is not beneficial. Chinese teachers
recognize that adults cannot learn a foreign language
merely by parroting. They must consciously master rules
to make inferences in studying new materials.

Since the aim of mastering a foreign language is to
communicate in society, material selected for classroom
practice must be determined by social needs. When students
arrive from abroad, they first want to express greetings,
and phrases used in daily conversation, and to master simple directions. Later they wish to read books and newspapers, to attend cultural activities, and to participate
fully in Chinese life. The topics spoken of in everyday
life in China such as politics, social activities, health,
production, therefore make up the main course content.
Students of science, technology and agriculture also want
to master the technical vocabulary of their specialty; content is determined in accordance with their needs.

In determining the complexity of materials, instructors
must consider the motivation of students as well as struc-
tural difficulties. For example, the sentence: Wǒmen yaò
liǎojiě Zhōngguó 'We want to know about China' is included
in the third lesson. Some instructors considered this
sentence too difficult syntactically because it has an
auxiliary verb; formerly such sentence types were introduced
much later in the course. But it is now found that such
sentences are easily assimilated because they are used
frequently by the students. If the course content meets
the needs of students, their motivation grows. In the
past instructors failed to give enough consideration to
social needs and to the interests of students, overemphasizing

instead the systematization of language science.  Now language classes are organized to reflect the social environment.

Accordingly, on the first day of instruction students
are taught sentences like: "How do you do," and "Welcome
to our Institute."  To be sure, instructors single out
the difficult tones and sounds of such sentences.  But
the former line between phonetics and syntax has been
broken.  It is now held that sounds cannot be taught in
isolation.  Moreover, phonetic drill concentrating on individual sounds is dull and boring; pure phonetic practice
fails to encourage students to use the language.

Sentences designed for syntactic analysis were previously centered on the classroom environment.  As a result, the students became deaf and mute as soon as they
left the classroom.  With the new approach and current
content, students have more opportunity to apply in their
daily lives what they have learned in class.  As a result
they actually have more phonetic practice than previously.
Since the syntax taught is systematically connected to
social needs rather than centered on the grammar itself,
the students are now able to converse inside and outside
the classroom.

Formerly the content of elementary language courses
was provided in short articles, with excessive literary
vocabulary.  Historical figures were too greatly emphasized.
Through the change of content to contemporary social situations, students can now talk about many topics after
three months of instruction.  They can also write compositions of a thousand words.

In short, students must know China, its communes, factories, May 7th Cadre Schools, and so on, in order to learn
Chinese.  No one can translate physics texts without a
knowledge of physics regardless of general language competence.  In the same way, one cannot learn to use Chinese
without a knowledge of China.  Accordingly it is best to
arrange courses in the Open Door Way, whereby students go
out among the people and talk with workers, peasants and
members of the People's Liberation Army.  Representatives
of these groups are also invited into schools to talk to
the students.  In effect, anyone who talks to a student
is his teacher.  The talk entitled 'Hanyu Zuowei Waiyu
Jiaoxue de Shijianxing Yuanze (Practice Principles of
Teaching Chinese as a Foreign Language)' by Mr. Lü Bi-song

at the Peking Language Institute has appeared in the
Journal of Chinese Linguistics (2:118-124).

4.  Classical Chinese

   Curiously, and quite unexpectedly, recent developments
in cultural policy appear to have brought about a widespread upsurge in the study of classical Chinese.  Even
the study of modern Chinese appears to be more broadly conceived than in recent years.  The result is that students
in schools, as well as the public at large through social
education channels, are receiving more formal instruction
about Chinese civilization than we had expected, and more
than has been described in writings on Chinese education
in the past ten years or more.
   In a typical middle school, the Seventh Municipal Middle
School of Zhengzhou, Second Year (eighth grade) students
in modern Chinese were using a new provisional textbook
promulgated by the provincial government's Education Bureau
in July, 1974.  The contents include a large proportion of
articles from recent Peking and Shanghai newspapers and
magazines, such as an editorial from the Red Flag and an
article from a Shanghai newspaper called "How to Write a
Good Report on a Commune."  The only items by named living
writers are a poem by Chairman Mao (and one by Guo Mo-ruo,
the President of the Academy of Science, in response to
which the Mao poem was written), and a long selection from
Deng Xiao-ping's early 1974 speech at the United Nations.
(In another province, Qiao Guan-hua's speeches at the UN
were used instead of Deng's, but he is the only current
official other than Chairman Mao to be included.)  Items
from the past include a selection from the Chinese translation of the "Communist Manifesto" and two selections
from ancient "Legalist" writings.  One is the section from
the chapter in the Taoist philosopher Zhuang Zi (Chuang
Tzu) called "The Brigand Zhi" in which the brigand exco-
riates Confucius for preaching an unrealistic altruistic
doctrine.  (The section is colorfully translated in Arthur
Waley's Three Ways of Thought in Ancient China, 1939, pp.
20-26, in the Doubleday paperback reprint.)  The other
selection in this textbook that draws on ancient classical
writings is the chapter "Geng fa" ("On changing the laws")
from the Book of Lord Shang.  Both essays are more than
2000 years old.  They appear in the unadulterated original

versions, accompanied by complete translations into modern
Chinese and by explanatory notes. The final item in the
textbook is a story by the father of modern Chinese literature, Lu Xun, who died in 1936. One class we visited
was reading another story by Lu Xun from a mimeographed
handout. This represents a broader and more interesting
range of reading materials than has characterized the recent textbooks known to us.

In the same school a Third Year class in classical
Chinese also was studying a new textbook issued last summer by the provincial Education Bureau. This was made up
almost entirely of selections from the newly defined category of Legalist writings of the past. The class was working on the chapter "Tian Lun" ("On Nature") from the third
century B.C. philosopher Xun Zi, usually considered in
the West to be a Confucian. (This chapter, no. 17 in the
Book of Xun Zi, is translated in W. T. Chan, A Source Book
in Chinese Philosophy, Princeton, 1963, pp. 116-124.)

The original text of the chapter from the ancient work
was accompanied by a good paraphrase in modern colloquial
Chinese, and by well-prepared notes identifying names and
explaining some allusions. The teacher, a native of Henan
province, graduated from Peking Normal University in 1957;
her Putonghua was excellent, with only a slight trace of
local intonation. All difficult new words and terms were
written on the blackboard in white chalk, followed by
alternate or complex forms plus pinyin in purple chalk.
The class was drilled on pronunciation and meaning, and
questions about the forms of the characters were answered
intelligently and fully. The class read the paraphrase
aloud, as a group. The teacher read the original text
aloud, one sentence at a time with repetitions, employing
a natural and lively sentence intonation to aid aural comprehension. Students as a group repeated after her. The
teacher discussed the meaning of the text, frequently
drawing passages from the original into her explanation,
thereby making the links between classical and colloquial
styles clear in the minds of the class. Although there
was little student participation on an individual basis,
as far as we observed here and in most other such classes,
the instruction was lively and effective. The class discussion turned entirely on the understanding of the fairly
difficult classical text, and the philosophical argument
which was presented as a rationalistic, proto-scientific

criticism of the ignorant and irrational views which Confucius and his school encouraged among the common people.

In this school, as in all other middle schools, colleges
and universities where instruction in classical Chinese
was observed, we asked whether students are expected to
write compositions in classical Chinese. The answer was
invariably that active command of classical written style
is not taught; no compositions in classical Chinese are
required.

Some years ago the study of classical Chinese had almost
disappeared from middle school curricula, and was slight-
ed in colleges. Now there is a renewed concern with classical Chinese under the current impetus to rediscover the
progressive Legalist thinkers of the past, who have been
engaged in a two thousand year long struggle against Confucian reactionaries. The popularization of this study of
ancient philosophy apparently is very new; no one visiting
China as late as 1973, to our knowledge, had yet picked
up any inkling that such a broad movement was about to be
launched. One could hardly have predicted that the criticism of Confucius would become so large a movement in
education that it would dictate the reopening of long-
closed chapters in Chinese intellectual history.

Everywhere the study of this problem dominates the
curriculum in Chinese. Under the slogan "carrying on education in an Open Door Way," so as to integrate learning
with the thought and experience of the workers, peasants
and soldiers, the study of Legalist thought has even been
taken to the factories and rural communes. In Sian, at
the Shaanxi Normal College, where there is a strong Department of Chinese, the students in classical Chinese
along with their learned senior professors have been studying the complete text of the Book of Lord Shang so as to
prepare an extensive critique and commentary, and have
been holding discussion sessions with factory workers to
seek their advice on how best to annotate the work. Elsewhere, we were told that a group of factory workers in
their self-study sessions had been writing a critique of
the Confucian work, the Doctrine of the Mean. In every
Chinese Department of every college or university we visited, projects of this kind are under way.

Professors tell us that the study of classical Chinese
has never been held in as much esteem since Liberation as
it is now, and that the study of classical writing is

burgeoning. Articles on Legalist thought dominate the
newly revived <u>Bulletin of Peking University</u> as well as
the publications of other institutions throughout the
country. The bookstores are now carrying a large line of
relevant publications, constituting almost the only current publications in the liberal arts. One can imagine
that the <u>Analects</u> of Confucius have not been so thoroughly
scrutinized by masses of the Chinese people since long before 1949. It appears that the past is being brought
fully into the informed consciousness of the Chinese people
to a degree not previously attempted by the present government.

Everywhere we were told that Confucius and the Confucian
mentality still are the principal enemy of progress. Therefore, only the head-on confrontation with all the lingering
influences of it will suffice to root it out. For example,
the private notebooks found in the study of Lin Piao after
his death are full of quotations from Confucius and Mencius,
showing that if his plot to capture the government had
succeeded, he would have restored Confucian doctrines.
We might have imagined that the government would have
chosen to repudiate all the past, Confucian and anti-Con-
fucian, for even the Legalists merit only partial approval.
They were progressive for their time, but they still represented an exploiting feudal ruling-group outlook. Yet
instead of closing the book on all the past, the government
has chosen to use a new interpretation of the past as a
tool to fight the lingering influences of past values.
They have chosen what traditionally has been the denigrated
tradition in Chinese social thought, have endowed it with
value, and have made it the instrument for opposing the
old but apparently still vital and dangerous Confucian
system. This suggests that despite the intellectual revolution of the 1920's and fifty years of Communist struggle
against Confucianism, the lingering power of the past still
is strong, so strong that only by using the past can they
combat the past.

It is too early to predict what quality the new study
may attain as intellectual exercise. But the earnestness
with which the teachers of classical Chinese prepare methods
and teaching materials suggests that the effort may reach
truly significant levels, and that it may deeply affect
education, scholarship, and cultural policy for a long
time. At the higher levels the new study of classical

Chinese not only is given the broad mission of serving
the masses, but also is specifially linked to the important
national efforts in archeology.  The discovery of extensive
Han versions of some pre-Han texts at Linyi in Shandong
and at Changsha in Hunan, announced during the past year,
including the earliest versions of those texts ever found,
has brought an element of great excitement to Chinese
studies in China and throughout the world.  These texts
are being prepared for publication, and young specialists
are being trained in the complex academic skills needed
for such work.

At Peking University, on October 23, Professor Zhu De-xi
talked briefly about the current work of preparing Han dynasty bamboo strip (<u>Han jian</u>) versions of ancient texts for
publication.  Two large finds of such texts are under study;
together they constitute the largest and most important
finds of actual Han period writing that modern scholars
have known.

One group of texts were found at Linyi, in Shandong,
in two graves dating from about 130 B.C., or early in the
reign of the Emperor Wu.  The texts found here include the
famous <u>Sun Wu on the Art of War</u> (<u>Sun Zi Bing Fa</u>) from the
sixth century B.C., and <u>Sun Bin on the Art of War</u>, written
by Sun Bin (ca. 380-320 B.C.), a lineal descendant of Sun
Wu.  The former text varies somewhat from extant versions;
the latter has not been known as an extant work, although
the title has been recorded.  Together they constitute
texts of over ten thousand characters.  Other military
texts, the <u>Liu Tao</u> and the <u>Wei Liao Zi</u>, in versions dif-
fering somewhat from extant versions, also were found.

The bamboo strips average 26.7 centimeters long and
less than one centimeter wide; they are very thin ("one
millimeter"), quite fragile, and contain one line of characters each.  The work of archeological salvage is being
done in the Shandong provincial museum.  After the strips
have been cleaned, treated, placed in glass tubes, and
photographed, they, or photographs of them, are turned
over to the Chinese Department at Peking University where
Professor Zhu and his staff work to reconstruct their original sequence, compare the texts with extant versions where
possible, and edit them for publication.

A larger group of texts was found at the site in
Changsha, Hunan, where three important tombs of the Western
Han period were unearthed.  The tombs in which the texts

were located date from 160 B.C.  The bamboo strips are
quite similar to those found in Shandong.  But in addition
to the texts in that form, a very large quantity of texts
written on silk were found.  The latter were written on
squares of silk on which red lines had been drawn first,
dividing the silk into strips resembling a group of bamboo strips placed side-by-side.  The texts were then filled
in with brush and ink.

The texts found at this site include a number of medical texts, two versions of the Lao Zi, an incomplete text
of the Zhan Guo Ce (translated by James Crump under the
title Intrigues of the Warring States) running to about
10,000 characters, of which one-third is not found in the
extant versions, the Book of Changes, military maps of
Hunan Province which may be the earliest maps in existence
anywhere, works on astronomy and astrology, and works with
illustrated charts explaining physical exercises.  Altogether the texts in the two forms, found in the three
Hunan graves, total about 120,000 characters.

The importance of the texts from the five tombs found
in the two provinces can be summarized as follows.  They
have brought to light more than 200,000 words of text in
early Han script, of which there have been few examples
heretofore; they provide many new books or new versions
of books; they supply scholars with important new materials
on early Han Legalist thought; they offer much material for
historical linguistics.

To speak of the last point, the texts are written in a
rather colloquial version, often using phonetic and other
borrowings.  The text variants thus may represent local
pronunciation which crept into the works because of oral
transmission, or they may represent loan graphs reflecting
standard early Han pronunciation.  Accordingly, they offer
much new evidence for the reconstruction of Han speech, as
well as a new body of evidence about that stage in the development of the script.

The Lao Zi texts have drawn particular attention throughout the scholarly world.  Professor Zhu noted that they
follow the same sequence as the Lao Zi to which reference
is made in Han Fei Zi (third century B.C.) in the chapters
"Jie Lao" and "Yu Lao."  Professor Zhu expects these texts
and others among those at present being analyzed to be
published within a year or two.

The China Pictorial, 9/1974, pp. 28-31 (Peking, English

language version) carries an illustrated article on the Shandong finds. A similar article on the Changsha texts appeared in the same periodical (1974:11).

The texts will aid the interpretation of the startling artifacts found in the Han burials of 160 and 130 B.C. Chinese archeology is one of the proudest achievements of the PRC, and justifiably so. Moreover, archeology has been widely drawn upon to prove that China's claims in the border disputes with Russia are valid, that Tibet has always been part of China, and the like. Archeology has demonstrated utility in China's quarrels with external foes, and it has been found a sharp weapon in establishing the correct line in the uses of history for domestic education. Archeology indeed may have been the key factor in the recent decision to draw on other aspects of the past in the broad attack on the lingering power of the domestic class-enemies, and to adjust the entire content of education in order to engage in that struggle armed with the correct knowledge of the past. Whatever its bases, current instruction in classical Chinese occupies a vastly different position in the educational system from that before the Education Revolution. Like the study of modern Chinese, it is intimately involved in the aim of education to serve proletarian politics.

## 5. The Teaching of English
## and Other Foreign Languages

## 1. Study of a Second Language

English is by far the most widely taught foreign language in the People's Republic. For example, at our visit to Middle School #15 in Peking on our second day in the PRC we were informed that of 41 classes into which the 2200 students are divided, thirty-nine are studying English. The two remaining classes, which are taking Russian, are at the senior level; one might then infer that next year English will be the sole foreign language taught in that school. Moreover, in Shanghai, where again English is the predominant foreign language, English instruction begins in the third grade of the primary schools, continuing through middle school. Inasmuch as the primary schools in Shanghai contain 1,500,000 pupils, and the secondary schools 1,200,000, one may conclude that many Shanghai children are learning English. We were also told that languages, such as Japanese, French and German, were taught in some of the schools. Other foreign languages as well are taught in the colleges, universities and language institutes.

Many citizens must also learn Putonghua as a "second language," as noted in the previous chapter. Moreover, the speakers of minority languages are also being taught Putonghua. And speakers of Putonghua who go to work with minority peoples learn their languages, as indicated in Chapter 8. There is accordingly a great deal of bilingualism in the PRC. Chapters 4 and 8 also deal with foreign language instruction; this chapter concentrates on the teaching of English.

The widespread stress on English is demonstrated by the use of English captions on all the exhibits in the Yenan Revolutionary Museum, and in the highly acclaimed Shanghai Industrial Exhibit. On the front of the exhibit building, •

a block-long sign in Chinese and English read: "Long live
Marxism, Leninism, Mao Tse-tung Thought."
     In light of the aims for foreign language teaching, as
discussed below, students are better able to discuss the
Legalists and Confucius than to comment on the life of the
people whose language they are studying.  An example of the
lack of information about the English-speaking world was
produced by the group of English majors from Langzhou University who met us in Yenan and were curious about the
blond hair of one of our delegates.  They wished to know
whether the color was due to old age or suffering.  We
were struck on the other hand by their expressions of
friendship to the American people.  We were also impressed
by their proficiency, especially their excellency in pronunciation.

2.   Foreign Language Teaching in Schools

      and Higher Institutions

     From the observations made by the Delegation, from
questions at the various institutions visited, and from
talking with people generally, it appears that foreign
language instruction is common in the major urban primary
schools starting with the third or fourth grades and continuing through the last year.  Some experiments with
foreign language teaching in the first and second grades
were also reported.  Foreign languages are taught in some
of the primary schools of communes near large urban centers such as Peking, Shanghai and Canton.  We were told,
however, that primary schools in the rural communes generally do not offer foreign language instruction.
     In every middle school foreign languages are offered
for the full five junior and senior years as part of the
standard curriculum.  It is not clear how far this pattern
extends into the rural communes; many of these currently
offer only three years of middle school education.
     All normal and general universities have foreign lan-
guage departments, but not all students are required to
take a foreign language.  Besides foreign language majors,
who take three years of a designated language, only those
students who need a foreign language for scientific or
technical training are likely to be enrolled in foreign
language classes.

In Peking and Shanghai the Delegation visited institutes specializing in foreign language training, and was
informed that similar institutes exist in other major
cities of China.

Although English is the predominant foreign language
also in higher institutions, we were unable to obtain
more than isolated information on language enrollments.
At Peking University, for instance, three of its seventeen departments concern foreign language and literature.
English is a division in the Department of Western Languages; 110 students are currently enrolled in the three
year program.  In Fudan University, English is taught in
the Foreign Language Department as are also Japanese and
German; besides these languages Russian and French are
taught in the Shanghai Normal University.

The Peking Language Institute, the facility in Peking
for teaching Chinese to foreign students, also has a foreign language department for Chinese students.  English,
Russian, French, Spanish, German, and Arabic are the foreign languages currently taught--with English having by
far the largest enrollment.  When the Shanghai Foreign
Language Institute was established in 1949, only Russian
was taught, but later English, French, German, Spanish,
Japanese and Arabic were added.  Now three additional languages are being introduced: Albanian, Greek and Italian.
It was reported that at institutes in some of the southern
cities Southeast Asian languages are also taught.

In primary and middle schools, language classes nor-
mally meet three class periods per week.  Foreign language
majors in universities and students in the specialized language institutes are enrolled for three years of semi-
intensive or intensive language training.

Primary and middle school classes have approximately
fifty students.  At the university level and in the foreign language institutes the classes are smaller, twenty
students or fewer.

We did not observe any English classes in regular sessions in the colleges, institutes or universities that we
visited.  The English classes we were to visit at Shaanxi
Normal College in Sian shifted to general discussion when
the opportunity arose to meet English-speaking visitors.
But these and other students as well as teachers discussed
the usual pattern of instruction.  The Sian students told

us that approximately seventy percent of the time was devoted to the study and practice of English. Two periods a day were spent in class and the balance of the time in small group practice and individual study. A good deal of emphasis is placed on practice in groups of three to five students. In those groups discussion in English focuses on assigned reading and on subjects of current political, economic, social and socialist revolutionary import. The class had recently been discussing agricultural and industrial production and the movement to criticize Lin Piao and Confucius. We were told that in those small groups the students criticize and help each other in a mutually supportive manner. When asked what English language material or literature they use in class for reading and discussion, they cited Red Star Over China by Edgar Snow, David Copperfield by Charles Dickens, the Voice of the People, the Monthly Review and the Manchester Guardian. While they have no language laboratory, they listen occasionally to the English instruction broadcasts by the Sian radio station.

At the Foreign Language Institute in Shanghai, classes consist of eighteen to twenty students, and the program is highly intensive. The daily pattern involves eight class periods: four in the morning, two in the afternoon, and two in the evening. In addition to language study, which occupies seventeen to twenty periods a week, students are required to take political studies, physical education, Chinese language, the geography and history of the country or countries whose language they are studying. Some students also study a second language.

In accordance with the effort to relate all education, including foreign language study, to the needs of the workers, peasants, and soldiers, and to better serve the needs of the society, the Shanghai Foreign Language Institute has added a "worker-teacher" of English to the staff. Like other instruction, foreign language teaching is carried out in the Open Door Way, according to procedures noted below.

3. Educational Philosophy

The pattern of English instruction at Peking University may illustrate what we found in varying degrees at other

universities and colleges.  Their views and approach were
explained to us by the English teaching staff.

Before the Cultural Revolution the teaching
content was rather redundant and scholastic.
Theory was cut off from practice.  Too much
attention was given to literature, to the
neglect of language learning.  The students
learned many rules about English, but they
had some knowledge of English literature,
and they learned many long and archaic words.
They might be able to recite Shakespeare, but
not express a simple idea in English.  For
example, they would say "to peruse a book,"
rather than "read a book."  A phrase in
Chinese describes this as "suffering from
deaf-mute disease."  To improve the situation we have instituted many changes since
the Cultural Revolution.

First, we try to combine our teaching
with present-day struggles and to relate
it closely with the realities of our socialist
society.  After finishing the basic course,
students often go out to practice and learn
English as well as to do practical work.
For example, a teacher will develop a lesson
devoted to a commune.  After students have
studied this text, they will go to the commune
to act as interpreters.  Sometimes they will
stay in the commune for two or three months.
While there, they learn the realities of
commune life and work from peasants.  At the
same time they continue their study of
English.  During such a period of field
study, they focus on agriculture.  They
learn to describe in English how a commune
is organized and how it functions.  They
also learn agricultural policy.  Moreover,
they undertake investigations, and report
on good deeds and accomplishments of workers
in the commune.  In this way they learn a
lot of practical vocabulary and useful sentence structures.  The students are eager

and well-motivated to learn those things in
order to express what they want to say while
working in a commune.

We organize our teaching materials by units.
For example, in addition to agriculture, units
focus on industry, medicine, education, and so
on.  This effort to put the students in real
life communication situations and expose them
to the realities of life of the workers, peasants
and soldiers is referred to as the Open Door Way
of Teaching and Learning.

Secondly, our teaching material is prepared
in accordance with the teaching of Chairman
Mao:  "Less but essential."  This means that
we want to teach the students the most important and essential things.  For example, in
teaching grammar we have tried not to give
the students many scholastic rules.  Instead,
we give them many sentence patterns or models.
Then the students are expected to do drills
based on the models, with grammatical explanations only as necessary.

Before the Cultural Revolution much emphasis
was placed on grammar.  Thus the students knew
about the language but could not use it properly.
Now we have no separate grammar course.  In our
text we limit grammatical explanations to those
which are needed by Chinese students learning
English.  In this way we combine theory and
practice.

Such educational philosophy was presented to us in various ways at all of the institutions we visited.  In visiting primary and middle school classes and talking to
university teachers and students we noted that concerted
efforts were made to apply these concepts.  At this time
it is still difficult to evaluate their success.

A few incidents may illustrate various ways in which
the Open Door Way, and the combining of theory and practice, are being carried out.

Several of the young people who were waiting on tables
at the Peking Hotel were English majors from Wuhan University in Hubei Province.  They had come to Peking for several

months to work in a situation where they could hopefully
practice their English with native speakers of English.
Several of the students enjoyed doing so with members of
the Delegation. At the same time, with the help of their
teachers they were developing materials based on conver-
sational situations encountered in a hotel for foreign
visitors; they were also conducting English classes for
the hotel staff.

When we visited the Industrial Exhibition in Shanghai,
students from the Foreign Language Institute attached
themselves to various members of the Delegation and acted
as guides through the Exhibition. Two of the guides had
been enrolled for two years in an English class run by
the Exhibition. Since their English had reached a degree
of proficiency, they were beginning to escort English-
speaking guests around the Exhibition. In this program
they have two classes in the morning, and self-study in
the afternoon.

In Canton, university and institute students were working as service people in the hotel, as guides in the Canton
Trade Fair, and at museums and tourist sites in the city.

The students from Fudan University who came with their
instructors for a very pleasant evening discussion tried
to tell us how their work with peasants in a commune improved their control of English. During their commune
work they learned the English names of plants and agricultural commodities, and practiced interpreting daily conversation between their classmates and the peasants on
the commune. They seemed very enthusiastic about the
benefits of these Open Door activities, but for the American linguists it was difficult to conceive that their
competence in English would benefit from such experiences
among monolongual speakers.

4. Motivation for Studying English

The question "Why are you studying English?" was put
to a number of students. The most common response was:
"To serve the Revolution." This response apparently comes
from a dialogue that appears in English texts. The dia-
log quoted below was taken from the Shanghai Radio English
text:

Lesson Two -

## We Study English for the Revolution

Wu:    What's that in your hand, Hsiao Wang?

Wang:   It's an English textbook. I'm studying English
        in our factory's spare-time school.

Wu:    That's good. Do you find English difficult?

Wang:   Yes, I do. But nobody is "born with knowledge."
        I must practice hard and learn English well.

Wu:    Yes, we must . We study English for the revolution.

Wang:   Yes, we do. Many people in the world speak English.
        We can use English as a tool and learn from the
        people of the world their revolutionary exper-
        ience.

Wu:    You're quite right.

Wang:   Marx says: "A foreign language is a weapon in
        the struggle of life." We must always remem-
        ber his words. Say, Hsiao Wu, you are a work-
        er student. You are studying English, too.
        Will you help me with my English lessons?

Wu:    I'd be glad to. Let's help each other.

In discussing the same question with university and language students, we received similar responses but with some
elaboration. For example, "We have much to learn from the
advanced scientific and technological development of the
English speaking people." Or, "English is a widely used
language and we want to be able to communicate with our
friends around the world." More specific objectives were
mentioned such as: "We need more English teachers, interpreters and translators;" and "We want to be able to talk
with and learn from our English-speaking friends who visit
China."

## 5. Teachers and Teacher Training

As a result of the rapid expansion of English teaching
in the PRC, there is a significant shortage of qualified
teachers. Few native speakers of English are reported to

be employed as language teachers in the foreign language
institutes and on university faculties. According to the
Delegation's observations, the competence of individual
teachers varies a great deal. Although the teachers of
English in the universities and specialized language institutes are generally more proficient in English than are
the teachers in primary and middle schools, we found several very competent teachers in the schools that we visited.

From our discussions at the two normal colleges we visited, it appeared that more attention is given to the development of language proficiency of prospective teachers
than to teacher training and methodology courses. It was
explained that acquiring an understanding of method and
procedure from their own experience as students would
assist them in meeting the problems other students would
experience in learning a foreign language. It was held
that instructors would learn how to teach through practice in the classroom. In Shanghai we were told that some
normal college foreign language majors spent three months
practice-teaching in the middle schools.

6.  The Type of English Taught and Teaching Materials

Knowing of the interest of the Chinese in standardizing
their own spoken language, the Delegation was interested
in finding out if a particular variety of English had been
selected as a standard. British English was obviously
preferred as a spoken model, although no one would say that
this was by policy direction. Preference for British English was generally rationalized on the grounds of established tradition and the phonetic standardization of the
Received Pronunciation. Moreover, it was felt to have
more acceptability and prestige throughout the world.

Text materials which members of the Delegation saw in
the classroom were sketchy as compared to foreign language
texts used in other countries. For example, Book I of the
English series used in one of the middle school systems
was a sixty-one page booklet containing thirteen lessons
listed as follows:

1.  Long Live Chairman Mao

2.  The English Alphabet

3.  We Wish Chairman Mao a Long, Long Life

4.  Our National Flag

5.  China

6.  The Red Sun

7.  Workers and Peasants Work for the Revolution

8.  The Best Weapon is Mao Tse-tung Thought

9.  Our Party

10. Mao Tse-tung Thought is the Beacon Light

11. Learn from the Working Class

12. Good Fighters of Chairman Mao

13. We are Chairman Mao's Red Guards

Each lesson included simple sentences on the subject, followed by a dialogue, as in Lesson 13:

We Are Chairman Mao's Red Guards

I

Chairman Mao, Chairman Mao!

You are the red sun in our hearts.

You are our red commander.

We are your Red Guards.

We are loyal to you.

II

Are you a Red Guard?

Yes, I am.

Is your sister a Red Guard?

No, she is not.  She is a Little Red Soldier.

Is your brother a Red Guard?

No, he is not.  He is a P.L.A. fighter.

After such texts, the English vocabulary is defined in Chinese, in a section entitled "New Words and Expressions." Thereupon notes on the text and phonetic aids to pronunciation are given, using IPA transcription to represent consonant and vowel sounds.

"Exercises" are based on common grammatical and sentence structures. Pictures are used to signal the response wanted from the student (e.g., What do you see in the picture? What are the Red Guards doing?). Sentences designed to demonstrate grammatical points or sentence structures are to be completed. Usually a selection for translation from Chinese to English is included in the lesson.

The back of the text contains a list of "Classroom English" expressions, such as:

> Let's study (read, recite) quotations from Chairman Mao.
>
> Chairman Mao teaches us "the working class is the leading class."
>
> Stand up.
>
> Sit down.
>
> Open your book at page ---.
>
> Read the text.
>
> Read after me.

Another list provides military expressions, such as:

> Cease fire!
>
> Stop, or we'll shoot.
>
> Don't move.
>
> Hands up!
>
> We are lenient towards P.O.W.'s.

And finally, an appendix provides an alphabetical list of vocabulary introduced in the text, somewhat over one hundred words. The series of six texts covers a vocabulary of approximately one thousand words.

The contents of Book VI lists both the subject of the lesson and the grammar as follows:

> 1. Lo Sheng-chiao (the story of a Chinese People's Volunteer who fought in Korea against the U.S. aggressors)

   2. Never Take Anything from the People

   3. A Million Serfs Have Stood Up (Tibet)
        Grammar: The Passive Voice

   4. Friendship Trees

   5. Yu Kung Removed the Mountains
        Grammar: The Infinitive

   6. The Song "The East Is Red"

   7. The First Time I Saw Karl Marx (after Paul Lafarge)
        Grammar: The Simple, Compound and Complex Sen-
        tences. The Adverbial Clause

   8. Chairman Mao Sends Me to School (I)

   9. Chairman Mao Sends Me to School (II)

  10. Energy

Members of the Delegation saw few examples of English
text material used in universities or in language institutes, for it was said to be "tentative" or "in an experimental state." Moreover, the preparation and publication
of textbooks is decentralized, so that texts may vary from
city to city. In response to questions concerning English
literature used in reading, writings by Edgar Snow, Anna
Louise Strong, Mark Twain, Charles Dickens, Eric Segal
(Love Story) were cited, and also English translations of
Marx, Lenin, Engels, and Chairman Mao.

In Shanghai we were told that advanced university students of English studied selected items from the New York
Times, the Economist, the Manchester Guardian, Time Magazine, Newsweek, U.S. News & World Report, the New Masses
and the Black Panther newspaper. These items, however,
were not seen in the open libraries.

Audio-visual aids are being used, often experimentally,
at the specialized language institutes and in the larger
universities, but not in middle or primary schools, where
the teachers are limited to simple devices such as pictures
and color-coded flash cards. The range and sophistication
of facilities varies considerably. We found audio-active
tape lab systems with monitoring capability in the foreign
language institutes we visited and at Peking University.
The institutes also have film projection facilities with

earphones at the seats and selective dialing of sound
tracks in several languages.  These facilities were also
to be used in training consecutive or simultaneous interpreters.

At the Peking Language Institute we were shown a film
on women trainees in the Chinese Air Force.  While the
film had not been prepared specifically for language instruction, foreign language tracks had been prepared for
comprehension purposes.  We were told that similar films
are also used as an exercise for students to describe, in
the language being studied, what is happening on the screen.

The Shanghai Foreign Language Institute had its own
recording facilities and film lab.  We were shown an animated film story entitled <u>The Cock Crows at Midnight</u> on
which foreign language sound tracks had been dubbed.  Both
the taped and filmed material were intended to support language training, and also to reinforce social or revolutionary objectives.

The use of audio-visual facilities, and their integration into the teaching system, were said to be in an experimental stage.  In keeping with this statement, we
found the use of these facilities roughly paralleled the
early stages of their use in American schools; they were
not fully integrated with the instructional materials or
with the system of instruction.

7.  Teaching Methods

Great stress is placed on practice in reading and
speaking.  Attempts are also made to avoid overly complicated and academic materials.  Rather than a mass of
texts, carefully selected materials are to be learned so
thoroughly that students can use them with flexibility in
a variety of situations.

In our observation of primary and middle school classes,
we found a general pattern of what the teachers referred
to as "classroom practice."  The teacher would give a word,
phrase or sentence in English and ask for choral repetition; individual students were then called on to read individually and to translate into Chinese.  The teacher
might then ask questions in English based on the text.
There was little spontaneous use of English by the students
or role playing of the dialogues.

With few opportunities to visit classes, it was difficult to evaluate the teaching methods described to us.
We did talk to some of the students as we toured the cam-
puses and met some of the graduates of the colleges, universities and institutes we visited.  On several occasions
we had informal discussions in English with individuals
or small groups of students.  We were generally impressed
with their pronunciation and use of grammatical structures,
but found the style and selection of vocabulary somewhat
stilted or textbookish.  The students were more confident
in discussing domestic Chinese production and political
matters than in talking about the society whose language
they were learning.  Apparently, very little, if any, attention is given to learning a foreign language in relation to the economic, social, political and cultural milieu
of the native speakers of those languages.
   An example of the focus on domestic matters is shown in
the type of topical reading materials developed for foreign language study.  One such supplementary reading selection is entitled "A Deepening of the Criticism of Lin
Piao and Confucius," which is apparently an English translation of a newspaper article.  Vocabulary items and
grammatical points with which students may have problems
are numbered and defined in Chinese.  The selection reads
in part as follows, with numerous references to annotations
in the student's text, as indicated by the many superscript
numerals:

The Party branch of anti-[1] chemical[2] warfare[3]
company of a PLA unit stationed[4] in Chekiang Province has launched[5] a massive[6] criticism of Lin Piao
and Confucius.  It mobilized[7] all members of the
company in a campaign[8] to do away with[9] supersti-
tions[10] and emancipate[11] their minds.---

---they used class analysis to compare[50] Lin
Piao's words and deeds, as well as[51] his programme
of counterrevolutionary coup d'etat[52], with what
Confucius advocated[53].  They saw that Confucius

proposed "self-restraint and a return to rites"
at a time when[54] the slave system was collapsing.
He sought[55] to return to the state system of Western Chou Dynasty, to restore the hereditary[56] system of slave-owning aristocracy[57], and to rein-
state[58] the decadent[59] slave-owning aristocrats[60]
who had lost their power and privileges[61]. Lin
Piao, trumpeting[62] Confucius' tune[63] at a time
when the proletariat had come to power[64], was
laying the groundwork for[65] a counterrevolutionary
coup[66].

Another selection dealt with a technical subject:
"Atoms and Electric Current." The purpose of this selection clearly was to provide scientific vocabulary such as
nucleus, positive electric charge, electrons, and names
of chemical elements.

Whatever the topic, the texts taught were selected for
their pertinence to the practical education favored since
the Cultural Revolution. The teaching methods are designed
to equip students with the language skills needed in their
practical pursuits.

## 8. English Teaching by Radio

Radio programs for teaching foreign languages exist only
for the teaching of English and Japanese. Every major
city has its English radio programs--an indication of the
interest in and spread of English as a second language.

In Shanghai we discussed the program with the staff of
the English department of the Normal University, who are
producing the materials and program with the cooperation
of the broadcasting station.

A new series of texts was published in June 1974 and is
available to participants through the publishing company
bookstores. It was reported that some 30,000 people in
the Shanghai area are studying with the program.

We were told that the materials had been developed after

extensive consultation with workers, peasants, and members
of the PLA.  To find out their needs and interests, the
materials were checked in draft form with potential users
before publication.  As with other English teaching materials, the contents of the lessons focus on subjects of
current interest, always with the purpose of serving the
goals of the Socialist Revolution.  Lessons cover such
subjects as "A Barefoot Doctor, We study English for the
Revolution (given above in Section 5.3), A Textile Worker, At the Station, A Letter, Visiting a Working Family,
and The Shanghai Industrial Exhibition."  More advanced
lessons are based on reading passages and dialogues on
such subjects as "Serve the People, Carry the Struggle
to Criticize Lin Piao and Confucius Through to the End,
Tachai Marches On, Growing Peanuts Scientifically, and
Recounting the Family's Revolutionary History."

Pronunciation is based on British English, but examples
of North American and Australian English are to be provided so that the listeners may learn to understand these
varieties as well as the Received Pronunciation.

Problems in radio teaching are acknowledged, particularly with pronunciation.  To overcome these, members of the
Normal University faculty and advanced English students are
sent to meet with groups of factory workers, soldiers or
peasants who are learning through the program.  Some of
the participants are also brought to the radio station
for discussions designed to benefit the listening audience;
these discussions focus on the problems that a speaker of
Chinese encounters in learning English.  There was some
evidence that secondary school and university students
were listening to the program to improve their comprehension.  On the other hand, when we asked whether people
listened to British or American broadcast language programs, we were told that these were not suitable to the
needs of Chinese students.

## 6. LEXICOGRAPHY


1. Dictionaries Available in the People's Republic

The Delegation visited a large number of bookstores in different cities, eager to see the available selection of dictionaries. The most common Chinese-Chinese dictionary, found in virtually every bookstore we visited, was the Xinhua Zidian (New China dictionary); ordinarily this work was available in a cheap paperback edition which most of us had not seen before. The Xinhua Zidian is a character dictionary rather than a word dictionary. Character dictionaries differ from word dictionaries in defining only single characters, though they include compounds as illustrative examples. Word dictionaries, on the other hand, have definitions both for single characters and compounds. The Xinhua Zidian is an outstanding example of Chinese lexicography. Widely sold in the United States, it is used extensively by both scholars and students, and apparently is the standard monolingual Chinese dictionary in China at the present time. The most recent edition appeared in 1972. It differs but slightly from earlier versions; here and there a definition has been altered for ideological reasons, illustrations have been eliminated, and some changes have been made in the appendices.

No new bilingual dictionaries were discovered. The standard English-Chinese dictionary, A Concise English-Chinese Dictionary, is seriously out-of-date. In view of the vast new emphasis on the study of English in China, the compilation of a new up-to-date English-Chinese dictionary would seem to be an urgent task. We heard of two efforts to produce new English-Chinese dictionaries, one at the Foreign Language Institute in Peking and the other at Fudan University in Shanghai.

Old stand-by lexicographical works such as the Guoyu Cidian (later abridged and republished as the Hanyu Cidian)

and Ci Hai were not found in any bookstore; in fact, we
did not see a single dictionary of character compounds
for sale anywhere.  Nor did we find any dictionaries of
the literary or classical language.  However, in the Fudan
University library, which is one of the two libraries we
visited, we saw these dictionaries and other traditional
reference works being used.

In short, few monolingual or bilingual dictionaries are
presently available on the open market in China.  The ones
that are for sale are either too limited in scope or too
out-of-date to serve current academic and social needs
effectively.  Accordingly, it is not surprising that lexicography is much on the minds of educators and that several dictionary projects are at present under way.

There are, however, many technical dictionaries, which
will not be discussed here.  Nor will we deal with Chinese-
Japanese dictionaries, or dictionaries involving other languages than English and Chinese.

The Chinese scholars and teachers with whom we talked
all recognize the importance of lexicography and the in-
adequacy of existing dictionaries.  Two distinct needs in
lexicography were discussed.  The first relates to the
study of classical Chinese; the second, to contemporary
written and spoken Chinese.

## 2.  Dictionaries of Classical Chinese

As noted further below in Section 4, several scholars
of Fudan University in Shanghai discussed with us the
need for new dictionaries of classical Chinese as well as
traditional lexicography.  By their report the struggle
between Confucianists and Legalists was not apparent in
the past to scholars such as themselves, nor to their pred-
ecessors.  As a result the linguistic dimensions of that
struggle were also overlooked.  For example, the important
Han period dictionary, the Shuo Wen Jie Zi of Xu Shen
(fl. A.D. 100), which has been a major influence on all
lexicography and classical scholarship, was a tool of the
Han Confucians in their anti-Legalist stand.  It defames
the First Emperor of the Qin (Ch'in) Dynasty; Xu Shen,
its compiler, was a representative of the slave-owning
landlord class of his time and was opposed to the peasant
class.  With Marxism, its reactionary character can be
detected while its positive qualities are still perceived.

All the old dictionaries are deficient in concentrating
on definitions drawing upon the Confucian writings, and
failing to note adequately the living speech of their own
time. This is also held to be true of the last great dictionary in the classical tradition, the K'ang-hsi Dictionary, dating from the early seventeenth century. In addition to reactionary thought content, dictionaries have
failed to note the colloquial literature and its living
usages, developing at least since the Tang Dynasty (618-
906 A.D.). Therefore they have failed to analyze or even
to record the developing relationship of single-graph word
to multi-graph term. Is Chinese monosyllabic? Is it an
isolating language? The nature of the script confuses
these issues, and the dictionaries have failed to help,
for they have ignored language change.

The professors at Fudan University went on to note that
at present, under the impact of the movement to criticize
Confucius, the number of persons in all walks of life who
are reading ancient texts has risen into the millions.
Since the broad masses are eager to criticize Confucian
writings and to evaluate the Legalist writers, they need
help. Dictionaries must be produced which present pronunciation simply and clearly; for this, pinyin is the most
useful vehicle. Scholars must deal analytically with the
problems of word and term. And examples must be selected
to present meanings which reflect present living conditions,
drawing on the realities of ordinary daily life, and correct in their thought content. Thus the Shanghai professors summed up the problems of dictionaries for classical
Chinese. But they did not indicate that they are engaged
in anything more than compilation of glossaries, or that
any effort of national scope was under way in this field.

## 3. Dictionaries of Contemporary Chinese

The problems of lexicography in modern Chinese parallel
those in classical Chinese. But instead of discussing de-
ficiencies in the influential ancient dictionaries, the
experts who spoke to us in Peking referred to improper content in dictionaries produced as late as 1965. The Cultural Revolution and the continuing revolution in education
have made virtually all scholarship, teaching materials,
and even dictionaries obsolete because of changing criteria
for correct political content. A group of thirty persons,

teachers and former members of the dictionary compilation
division of the Commercial Press, are at work completing
revision of a new popular dictionary designed to meet a
broad need.  This work is being done under the auspices
of the Peking Educational Circles.

The dictionary will be aimed at middle school level
users.  A preliminary draft of the dictionary has been
completed.  It contains 12,000 single character main entries and about 20,000 compounds entered under the single
characters.  The dictionary will be in phonetic order of
the main entries, but pronunciation will not be indicated
for the sub-entries.  Classical meanings will be given
only when they are still used in the modern written language.

Material for this dictionary has been gathered from
Chairman Mao's works, Renmin Ribao, Hongqi, and middle
school textbooks.  Emphasis is placed on material that
has appeared since the Cultural Revolution.  In addition
to the above-mentioned material, use was made of the
Xiandai Hanyu Cidian put out by the Commercial Press in
1973 (see below); this includes some lexical data taken
from modern literature.

Many simple compounds have been omitted intentionally,
since the compilers felt that most people would not look
up such items in a dictionary; examples are gāoxing 'happy' and róngyi 'easy'.  Particular attention has been given
to those entries which have philosophical or ideological
import.  There will be both explanations and critiques of
meaning; these will draw on Marxism and the Thought of
Mao Tse-tung.  An example offered to us is the critique
of the word rén 'human being, man, person'.  To the basic
definition that man is the animal capable of using tools,
possesses the capacity for thought, and can perform labor,
the critique will add the information that all persons
have a "point of view" so that there is no such thing as
"abstract man."  "Person" can be understood only in relation to class status and social context.

The lexicographers criticized earlier dictionaries for
including long-winded, pedantic definitions of everyday
words.  They provided one humorous example: the verb dūn
'to squat' formerly was defined as 'to bend the legs as
much as possible so that the [posture] resembles sitting,
but without the buttocks touching the ground'.  They considered such a definition ridiculous because everyone

knows what d$\overline{u}$n means to begin with.  All that is necessary
is to identify the word by saying something like "the d$\overline{u}$n
which occurs in the phrase d$\overline{u}$nzai dìshang 'to squat on the
ground.'"

In addition to such content, specialized content is
being processed through boards of experts, for example in
medicine, party organization, and the sciences.

The annotation work is the most time-consuming part of
this task, for not only must the thought content of the
definitions and the critiques be freed of all error, and
the specialized knowledge of technical experts included,
but the annotations must also be reviewed by teams of workers and peasants.  These persons, approached through their
work units, gladly offer their help, expressing their cultural needs and reflecting their realistic points of view.
Only when all of their inputs have been incorporated can
an entry be completed.  The work is now in a final revision
stage, and it is hoped that a final product can soon be
sent to press.  No timetable however was indicated.

This group of lexicographers informed us that another
such project was under way in the dictionary compiling
division of the Commercial Press in Shanghai, and also at
other places, including some other dictionary efforts in
Peking.  Yet, although products of earlier phases of such
work, undertaken a number of years ago, have been exchanged,
there is at present no communication among such groups, and
no overall coordination of their various efforts.  The lack
of coordination may be illustrated by our experience in
Shanghai.  When we asked to meet the persons working in
the dictionary compiling division of the Commercial Press,
we were told that it had been transferred to Peking more
than twenty years ago.

At Peking University we were told that the work of compiling the Xinhua Zidian, published first in the mid-sixties,
revised in the standard edition of 1965, and now sold in a
revision dated 1971, was done primarily at Peking University, as was the work of compiling the new Chengyu Cidian,
recently put on sale.  These same persons told us that the
Xiandai Hanyu Cidian, a larger dictionary of terms intended
to accompany or supplement the small Xinhua Zidian, is still
under compilation and might be published at a later date.
A week or so later in Fudan University Library, quite for-
tuitously as it turned out, a member of the Delegation
noted a published copy of that work on the reference shelf.

It is a fairly large work containing 1400 pages of which
1385 are devoted to actual entries.  The dictionary contains 53,000 entries, all given in phonetic order.  Pronunciation is included both for single characters and for
compounds.  According to the front matter, it was compiled
by the Dictionary Compilation Office (Cidian Bianjishi)
of the Commercial Press in Peking, and published for the
Academy of Science.  It was printed in May 1973, as a
"tentative edition" (shiyongben).  Perhaps we were not
told of this printing because it still is not a final
version.  We were unable to acquire a copy of it.

In Shanghai we were able, however, to buy copies of a
new Workers, Peasants and Soldiers Dictionary (Gongnongbing
Zidian), roughly the size of the Xinhua Zidian.  Published
in 1973, it was compiled by a lexicographical group at the
May 7th Cadre School for the fields of journalism and publishing in Shanghai.  Its contents, format and scope are
all very similar to those of the Xinhua Zidian.

4.  Views on Available Dictionaries and Prospects

        for the Future

On the evening of November 8, members of the Fudan
Chinese Department came to our hotel, and among other
things discussed the Xiandai Hanyu Cidian dictionary with
some of us.  They consider the dictionary up-to-date in
the spheres of phonology and character simplification.
All entries are in pinyin; neutral or atonic syllables
are indicated.  On the negative side, however, since the
dictionary was put together before the Cultural Revolution,
it contains numerous inappropriate entries and examples.
Moreover, many recent political and technological terms
have been omitted.  An instance of an inappropriate entry
is provided by shèngrén 'sage', which is further defined
as 'a person superior in wisdom'; the example given is
"Confucius was a sage."  This entry is inappropriate on
two grounds: the concept 'sage' is no longer considered
a positive one, and Confucius is certainly not to be held
up as a model of anything.  Other entries represent erro-
neous or outmoded ideas; examples are tiānmìnglùn 'pre-
destination', nòngzhāng and nòngwǎ (obsolete expressions
used for the birth of boy and girl children respectively).
Among the new terms omitted, the following were cited:

dàpīpàn 'mass criticism', xuéxíbān 'study class', jīguāng 'laser', chìjiǎoyīshēng 'barefoot doctor', zhēnjiǔ mázuì 'acupuncture anesthesia'.

The dictionary was also criticized for containing too many Peking localisms and too many forms with the -r suffix, also a feature of the Peking dialect.

At present the Xiandai Hanyu Cidian is being reviewed by workers, peasants and soldiers. It was not clear to us when this dictionary would become available to the general public.

The group from Fudan gave a very favorable critique of the Gongnongbing Zidian. Whereas the Xiandai Hanyu Cidian contains many inappropriate examples, the Gongnongbing Zidian was felt to be quite acceptable in this regard. It was compiled after the Cultural Revolution, and consequently it reflects the current ideological position. One example of this sort of difference was given: in the Xiandai Hanyu Cidian, rú 'Confucian' was defined as 'an ancient Chinese philosophical school founded by Confucius which advocated benevolence and righteousness'. This definition, it was pointed out, fails to take into account the present view of Confucius and his school of thought. The Gongnongbing Zidian defines the same word as 'a school of thought in Ancient China, founded by Confucius, which represented the interests of the exploiting class'. Apparently this sort of ideological aggiornamento is necessary in current lexicographical work.

Our conclusions about lexicography are that the work is going on in many places, to meet immediate needs for both monolingual Chinese and bilingual dictionaries. We heard of efforts on English-Chinese, Chinese-English and various other sorts of bilingual dictionaries. We found no evidence, however, of national coordination. Political correctness of content is apparently the most difficult problem facing general lexicographical work.

If a base exists for coordinated and large-scale work in lexicography, we were unable to learn of it. People in Shanghai, for example, had never heard of the dictionary project which we were briefed on in Peking. The people in Peking, likewise, seemed quite unaware of efforts in Shanghai. But this is just one facet of the lack of coordination and the decentralization of the academic world in China. At various times we inquired about possibilities of cooperation between the United States and the People's Re-

public in the area of Chinese and English lexicography.
It appeared to us, that while there was some interest in
an exchange of materials, any exchange of personnel was
unlikely for the foreseeable future.

# 7.  LANGUAGE PATHOLOGY:
## EXPERIMENTAL RESEARCH


## Introduction

In the last few years in the United States there has
been an increase in interdisciplinary research involving
linguists and communication engineers, speech pathol-
ogists, aphasiologists, neuroanatomists, neurophysiologists, cognitive and physiological psychologists, and
even other specialists.  These interdisciplinary activities
reflect, on the one hand, a growing awareness on the part
of these other disciplines of the contributions linguistics may make to investigations of both normal and ab-
normal speech production and perception.  Attempts to develop automated speech understanding systems now rely on
syntactic, semantic, and phonological linguistic input
as well as on the more traditional acoustic and phonetic
analysis of the physical signal.  Aphasia research, as
well as the diagnosis and treatment of aphasia patients,
is more and more based on linguistic theoretical foundations.  Work with the deaf includes efforts to understand
the linguistic structure of sign language and its similar-
ities to and differences from spoken language.  On the
other hand, linguists are recognizing that they have much
to learn from the research in these areas in their attempts
to develop a viable theory of human language.  In seeking
to define the class of possible languages and the grammars
which underlie them, investigators are proposing explanatory as well as descriptive theories.  Aphasia data,
child language acquisition studies, split brain and hemi-
spheric lateralization experiments are viewed as providing
evidence in testing alternative linguistic hypotheses concerning the psychological reality of grammars.  For these
reasons, the Delegation was interested in seeing what if
any parallel efforts were being pursued along these lines
in the PRC.

Since these research efforts are comparatively recent, it is not surprising that our requests to meet with acoustic physicists, engineers, brain surgeons and neurophysiologists in China presented some problems for our linguistic hosts. Our discussions with non-linguists or with scholars in non-language areas were therefore very limited. The summaries which follow are based solely on two visits to schools for the deaf, one discussion with a group of four medical neuroanatomists and researchers, and on the impressions we drew from the more general meetings with linguists and language experts. Many of our questions remain unanswered. What follows should be viewed as highly tentative.

## 1. Phonetic Research

### 1.1 Acoustic Analysis and Synthesis

We did not meet with any researchers in the area of acoustics. From what we could gather there is little cooperative effort between linguists and acoustical engineers in the PRC. None of the linguists attempted to inform us where such research was being conducted or who were the individuals involved in the investigation of the physical properties of speech. At the Shanghai Industrial Exhibition on the other hand we saw an artificial larynx which is quite different from the one produced in the United States. Yet we are not certain where the main centers of acoustic research are, although an Institute of Acoustics exists in Peking as part of the Academy of Sciences. Nor were we able to determine whether Sheng-Xue Xue Bao (Acoustics Bulletin) is still being published. Our information concerning this field dates back to 1965. Four articles from that journal, published in 1965, have been translated and distributed by the Joint Publication Research Service— Clearinghouse for Federal Scientific and Technical Information of the U.S. Department of Commerce. These papers explicitly reveal research interests in 'intelligibility' studies, speech transmission systems, speech synthesis and automatic speech recognition. The titles of these articles and a brief abstract of the first, are presented to indicate the direction of the research at that time.

'Standard Frequency Spectra of the Chinese Language' by Ma Ta-yu and Chang Chia-lu. (Author's affiliations not given) Sheng-hsueh Hsueh-pao, Vol. 2, No. 4, 1965, p. 217.

Standard Frequency spectra for Chinese were determined
using mean frequency spectra previously obtained by Hsu
Huan-chang (Sheng-hsueh Hsueh-pao [S-h H-p] 2, 1965, 203).
The mean frequency spectra were modified by smoothing the
lower band and by replacing the high frequency band by a
straight line with a slope of 12 db/"multiple frequency
range." Total sound intensities were determined by a
summation process and converted into sound pressure levels.
A sound pressure level of 69 db at one meter from a speaker's lips was considered the standard condition. The
authors conclude that an error of less than 2 db results
from comparison between the standard and actual frequency
spectra.

'The Mean Spectral Characteristics of Ten Vowels
of Standard Chinese (Putonghua)' by Hsu Huan-chang
[Acoustical Institute, Chinese Academy of Sciences]
S-h H-p, Vol. 2, No. 1, March 1965.

'The Pitch Indicator and the Pitch Characteristics
of the Tones in Standard Chinese', by Lin Mao-tsan
[Institute of Philology and Linguistics, Chinese
Academy of Sciences], S-h H-p, Vol. 2, No. 1,
March 1965, pp. 8-15.

'Vowel Identification in Relation to Syllable Du-
ration', by Liang Chih-an [Shanghai Institute of
Physiology, Chinese Academy of Sciences], S-h H-p,
Vol. 2, No. 1, pp. 20-23

In these articles a number of references are made to
papers, monographs, and books on acoustics written by foreign scholars from the United States, Japan, the Soviet
Union, Sweden, Germany, etc., and to publications such as
those of the Acoustical Society of America, the Phonetic
Society of Japan, the International Congress of Phonetic
Sciences, and the Soviet Journal of Physiology.

Because of our lack of contact with scholars in this
field we were unable to determine whether work along the
lines indicated above has continued, and, if so, what
accomplishments have been made in this area. The data
presented in the few papers translated are valuable for
those interested in acoustic analysis and synthesis, particularly because of the work reported on the tones and
phones of spoken Chinese. It would be very helpful to
receive additional publications and to have future

exchanges with colleagues working in this area in China.

## 1.2  Physiological/Articulatory Phonetics

We have even less information about this area of research since we did not have access to any publications published since 1949 and prior to our visit.  If there is any experimental research, utilizing instrumental techniques, on the physiology of speech production, it is not carried out by phoneticians or linguists in such places as Peking University, Fudan University, the Peking Language Institute, or the Central Institute for Nationalities.  Yet such research may be centered in medical and physiological institutes.

The linguists and language specialists are, however, interested in phonetic descriptions of the dialects being surveyed and of the national minority and foreign languages being taught.  Phonetic differences between Putonghua and the other dialects provide a major concern.  The framework on which descriptive studies of this kind is based appears to be traditional IPA.  The descriptions and vocal tract diagrams of English sounds in an English textbook which we purchased are like those presented by Daniel Jones and Ida Ward.  Concerns of many phoneticians in the United States and Europe having to do with a universal set of phonetic features, phonetic explanations for "natural" synchronic and diachronic processes in phonology, the relationship between phonology and phonetics, and so on, did not arise in our discussions, possibly because such questions do not appear to have any immediate practical applications, that is, they do not relate directly to the popularization of Putonghua, or dialect descriptions, and so on.

But phonetic alphabets, IPA as well as pinyin, are widely used in the teaching of foreign languages, in the teaching of Chinese to foreigners, in the popularization of Putonghua, and in the teaching of the deaf to speak.  Students throughout China, from primary school on up, are exposed to phonetic transcriptions and explicit descriptions of speech sounds to a far greater extent than are our students.

We were unable to determine the extent of phonetic training of the students doing field work on Chinese dialects.  Clearly they are taught to transcribe, since this

is the main method of data collection. We were told that
for the most part the informant sessions are not tape recorded. How narrow or broad these transcriptions are we
could not judge. Since we were led to believe that there
are no specific classes in phonetics, it is likely that
students, with just a minimum of training in transcription,
learn their phonetics in the field. The emphasis is clearly on practical phonetics as opposed to theoretical phonetics.

2.  The Language of the Deaf

We visited two schools for the deaf, one in Peking and
one in Shanghai. The information summarized below was
obtained from the introductory remarks of the leading members at each school, and from the answers to questions
which we raised in the discussions. Our impressions of
the classes we visited are also included.

2.1  Third Deaf-Mute School in Peking

This school was founded in 1958. It is an eight-year
old school, with 280 students, ranging in age from nine
to seventeen, studying in fourteen classes. The entrance
age is from nine to fourteen. Most of the students live
in the school but go home for weekends. The fee for room
is five Yuan ($2.50), tuition is 2.5 Yuan, but for students
from the rural areas, 1.5 Yuan per semester. Food costs
are ten Yuan a month. Upon graduation students are assigned work by the state, usually in factories, such as
those producing toys or handicrafts.
In keeping with the Educational Revolution, the over-
riding principle is to help the students develop morally,
intellectually, and physically. Since the Cultural Revolution, and especially in the movement to criticize Lin
Piao and Confucius, the school has criticized and repu-
diated Liu Shao-chi's counterrevolutionary, revisionist
line and now is run in the Open Door Way. To help the
students integrate themselves with the workers, peasants,
and soldiers, and combine their book knowledge with practice, two small factories have been established in the
school--a carpet factory and a sewing workshop. In addition, the students are organized to go out to factories
and the countryside to learn from the workers and peasants

and to participate in industrial and agricultural production. Workers and peasants are also invited into the school. Outside of class, extracurricular activities are organized. Coaching teams help the students with self-study. Sports and cultural activities are provided.

We were told that since the Cultural Revolution a new type of relations between students and teachers has been established, which were defined as 'democratic, revolutionary, and unitary'. During the Cultural Revolution, Mao Tse-tung Thought Propaganda teams, organized by PLA units and workers of the city, came to the school to lead the teachers and students in the Educational Revolution, and also to treat the students. 'In order to help the students get relief from their suffering' the members of the Propaganda Team went out to learn from the experiences of other units. They also practiced acupuncture on themselves and each other prior to administering acupuncture treatments to the students.

Some of the students in the school are congenitally deaf; others became deaf due to illness or trauma. Both groups are faced with the problem of communicating with others in society. The school is equally concerned with hearing improvement and cure, and with speech training.

Acupuncture is the main method of treatment. We were told that after a certain period of treatment, the hearing of all students is improved, but the degree varies considerably. Some students, who prior to treatment could hear sounds only at a distance of six meters, can now hear at twenty, thirty, forty, and more meters distance. We were not told the methods of measurement, although it was reported that instrumental methods were used. A more impressionistic method is utilized in the classrooms where from different distances the teacher speaks to a student whose back is turned and the student is asked to repeat what was said. No statistics were provided as to the number of students whose hearing was improved with treatment, nor the extent of the improvement. The doctor at the school reported that there was between fifty and seventy percent improvement, with the greatest improvement occurring in the spring. When asked why this was so, she replied that it was due to the Yin-Yang principle; in spring the energy force, qi, is released. After the Propaganda Team was withdrawn, the school's doctor, together with the teachers, administered acupuncture. Other

traditional medicines are used, but we were not informed
about these.

Students whose hearing is considered sufficiently improved are sent to regular schools.  It is believed that
remaining at the school for the deaf will be detrimental,
since they will continue to use sign language and have
less motivation to use speech.  Past experience has shown
that the oral communication of students is greatly improved after six months in a regular school.  One student
through great effort improved his speech to such a degree
that he was able to enlist in the navy, where he now serves
in the communications section.

When hearing is improved with the use of acupuncture,
training in articulatory phonetics and articulation begins,
since restoration of some hearing ability by itself does
not result in the ability to produce speech.

In this Peking school (but not in Shanghai, as noted
below) the congenitally deaf seem to show greater response
to acupuncture than do the postnatal deaf.  A number of
problems remain in the efforts to affect 'cures'.  It was
pointed out that some students who at first show improved
hearing retrogress, particularly during periods of tension,
excitement, or anger.

Hearing aids are used very infrequently.  For the profoundly deaf at birth they seem to have little effect.
It was acknowledged that for those children with some
hearing, the hearing aids may be of help despite the dis-
tortion.  Since, however, the emphasis is on speaking and
cure, the distortions make for difficulties, and students
begin to rely on the aids rather than being motivated to
improve their hearing with no auxiliary devices.  We saw
no children with hearing aids in the schools, although we
did see adults wearing aids at various places in China.

A national unified finger-spelling system, based on
pinyin (with four signs to represent the tones, the gestures iconically similar to the diacritic tone marks) was
promulgated in 1963 and is now used in addition to the
traditional sign language used before Liberation.  Both
systems were demonstrated by one of the teachers and a
student.  Although sign language is used in the school,
emphasis is placed on oral communication with understanding
aided by lip reading.  We were told that in the classroom
the teacher first uses speech.  If this is not understood,
children are instructed to try to understand the sentence

by lip reading.  As a last resort, sign is used.
   The hearing parents of deaf children do not generally
learn sign language, but often use 'natural' signs to
communicate with their children.  When more than one deaf
child is in a family, parents often learn sign from their
children; but no efforts are made by the school or the
state to provide classes in sign for hearing parents.
Among themselves children use sign language rather than
finger-spelling.
   The reason given for the emphasis placed on listening
and speaking was the concern that the children learn, if
possible, to communicate in the hearing world.  It is believed that if only sign is used, or used excessively, the
children will not be motivated to understand and use speech,
and this will affect their development.  We were further
told that to help in learning to understand spoken Chinese,
single sentences are drilled each day.  If one day is not
enough, additional days are used for drill.  There was no
response to the question concerning the fact that for the
most part we are confronted with novel sentences never
heard before, and that as a result such drills may be of
no help outside the classroom.  Here is clearly one area
where a particular theory of language determines practice.
   Cultural and social activities are arranged for the
students of the school, such as visits to exhibitions,
films and athletics.  But no special arrangements are
made for the deaf.  When required, teachers act as interpreters in sign at these events.
   After graduation the children are assigned work which
is particularly suited to them.  Special considerations
are given to the deaf and to all handicapped; no discrimination of any kind exists, according to our hosts.
   We visited a class where acupuncture was being administered.  The needles were inserted behind the ear as well
as in front of the ear.  The students did not appear to
be frightened or in any pain, although they were not particularly animated.  There was little talk in this class
and we did not observe any sign language being used.
   We also visited the carpet factory where there were
about twenty-four boys and girls weaving carpets.  The
instructor was a graduate of the school and was herself
deaf.  We noticed a much greater use of sign language between the teacher and the students and among the students
themselves.  This teacher, and the fine arts teacher, were

the only deaf teachers in the school.

We then visited two classes, the first, a third grade class in articulation training and the second a class in the Chinese language.

## 2.1.1  Articulation Training Class

The teacher was drilling the students on tones and words beginning with h, e.g., hua, hui and han in all four tones. These were printed on the blackboard in phonetic transcription with the h in red chalk and all the tones marked by diacritics. At the front of the room were diagrams of lateral sections of the vocal tract, as can be found in most phonetic books, showing tongue and lip positions. The teacher first said the vowel and the students repeated it back in chorus. Then the words were repeated, and thereupon the entire contrastive series in this way. The children then held strips of paper in front of their mouths as they attempted to produce the aspirate h. Following the collective choral drills, individual students were called on and went to the front of the room where the teacher would try to correct the pronunciation, calling attention to lip positions, tongue positions, pointing to herself and the children's lips and throat, and to the diagrams. There was understandably great difficulty with the contrasting tones since laryngeal control is more difficult to describe than supra-glottal articulations. The teacher told us that the pronunciation abilities correlated closely with the hearing abilities. Some of the students in the class were profoundly deaf--with no hearing at all. Most of the students, however, had some hearing, even those who had none before treatment had commenced. The teacher used finger-spelling in her attempts to help the students, and some regular sign in her descriptions of the speech sounds.

## 2.1.2  Chinese Language Class

In the language class, sentences were written on the board. The teacher would read them and the whole class would repeat them after her in chorus. Even to those of us who knew no Chinese it was clear that many, if not most, of the students were not repeating the sentences, but were vocalizing syllables, seemingly in a somewhat random way.

The teacher seemed aware of this but continued the drill and encouraged all vocalizations. The class was noisy, which was interesting for a class of deaf students. All of the students seemed to be trying very hard. Individual students were called on to read the sentences which to a great extent were read in a list, sing-song intonation, with one word after the other, each produced with great force and intensity. There was much pitch variation over a small range, but not necessarily in keeping with the target tones or normal sentence intonation. Again we did not notice the teacher using much sign language except in the attempt to correct individual phones.

The teacher then conducted a drill which involved understanding of spoken speech. She would read an individual word and students who raised their hands would be called on to come to the board and point out the word read. There was great variation among the children in their ability to repeat by rote and to understand.

## 2.2  Shanghai School for the Deaf

This school, one of ten schools for the deaf in Shanghai, was established in 1966. Of the 125 students, one-third are congenitally deaf. Unlike the Peking school this is not a boarding school; the children live in the area close by. Most students enter when eight years old, and spend eight years in the school with an additional two years at a technical training school. Following graduation, they are assigned to work for which they have been specially trained.

The curriculum of the school is the same as that in regular schools: mathematics, geography, history, Chinese, drawing, physical culture, and Marxist-Leninist Mao Tse-tung thought. Extracurricular activities in athletics and culture are organized.

When a new student enters, he is given a physical examination and a first treatment plan is established. If following this first plan little or no improvement in his hearing results, a further plan is worked out. We were not informed on details of the treatment except for the fact that all students receive acupuncture. Acupuncture treatments were initiated at the end of 1968 by a medical team of the PLA. The team, in addition to treating the children and organizing the teachers to study Mao Tse-tung thought, also taught the teachers how to administer acupuncture. After the army team left, doctors from the district hospital were assigned to the school, and one of the army doctors remained as part of the staff.

We were again told that all students show some hearing improvement with the treatments, but great variation still exists in the degree of cure. Audiometric tests are administered twice or three times each term to determine the extent of improvement. In addition, the teachers administer less controlled tests, such as striking a hollow box, or bell, or clapping at different distances from the students.

The earlier treatments are started, the better the results. Unlike the report at Peking the treatment seems equally effective for congenital and postnatal deafness. It was reported that sixty percent of the students showed improvement in grade two. The first grade students were too new to evaluate. Because treatment is not as effective among the higher grade children, the emphasis on oral language is in the early grades, although pronunciation training continues. In the first two grades less sign is used than in the later grades. From grade three up, all instruction of the content courses is in sign language.

In 1969, out of the 107 students, thirty-seven students with better hearing/speaking ability were selected to attend regular school. Later, others were sent. Altogether, forty-three students are now attending regular school. The hearing ability of most of these students has improved considerably and they seem to be keeping up with the normal students. Some of the students who appear to have greater difficulty are individually coached.

The two forms of sign language are employed, each for a different purpose: finger-spelling, primarily to aid in the teaching of articulation; regular sign, as the medium of instruction. All the teachers are taught both forms of sign language, as well as acupuncture, before being assigned to teach classes. The teachers are selected from among the best primary school teachers and from graduates of normal schools.

Although there are no special classes in sign for

parents of deaf children, the teachers sometimes visit the homes to instruct the parents in sign. This is particularly done for the parents of the older children who have greater difficulties in understanding and using spoken language. Many of the children come to the school not knowing the standard sign language; this is then taught to them.

In answer to a question concerning the possibility of university training for the deaf, we were told that the main priority at present is the education of all the deaf. Before Liberation only the few deaf children of the rich received any education. Now all deaf children are educated and a vast number of schools have been established. It is hoped that with improved medical treatment and preventive measures the number of the deaf will decrease. For example, many cases of deafness resulted from smallpox and meningitis; but with the immunization program and medical treatment such cases are now minimal. The plan is to reduce the number of schools in Shanghai from ten to four by 1980, and to one by 1985.

We attended a class in phonetic articulation training and a class in the Chinese language. These were conducted similarly to those we visited in Peking. We also attended a sixth grade geometry class, which was taught in the 'total-communication' method. The teacher signed and spoke while she signed. The students primarily answered in sign. We also were entertained by a group of students. A few of these students are now attending regular school or were graduates of this school. They recited, individually and in chorus, sang solos or choral compositions, danced, and performed on musical instruments.

## 2.3 Summary

(1) After Liberation many schools for the deaf were established which now provide education for all deaf children.

(2) The emphasis is on cure and training in spoken language, but both a finger-spelling system and the older Chinese sign language are used in the schools. In Shanghai all the upper grades in schools for the deaf are taught in sign. We do not know whether this is also true in Peking.

(3) The major treatment administered is acupuncture, which is reported to improve hearing from fifty to sixty percent. Statistics were very meager, and the measurement

and evaluative methods not always clear.  We were of course
unable to judge the effectiveness of the acupuncture treatments.  Dr. Samuel Rosen, who has visited the PRC four
times, has attempted to replicate the treatments in the
United States, and reports that he has been unable to find
any improvement (Acupuncture and Chinese Medical Practices,
Volta Review, Vol. 76, No. 6 (1974), pp. 340-350.)  It is
not possible to judge the reasons, since the methods of
application, the social pressures, the motivations and
so on are very different.

        (4)  Hearing aids are used infrequently, primarily
because of the emphasis on 'cure'.  There is also concern
that the distortions of the sounds will prohibit articulatory development, and fear that a reliance on hearing
aids will inhibit the efforts to improve attentive listening and understanding without auxiliary devices.

        (5)  The teaching methods regarding language training
appeared to be primarily by rote repetition.  But the teachers in both schools seemed to be highly dedicated, patient,
warm, and encouraging, and the children were attentive,
involved, and appeared quite happy.  We were told that only the best teachers are selected for schools for the deaf.

3.  Neurolinguistic Research

    On the evening of November 7, a few members of our
Delegation met with a group of four members from the
Shanghai Physiology Institute and the Hua Shan Hospital
of Shanghai.  The visiting group included:

        Xu Bing-fan, Shanghai Physiology Institute,
            anesthesiologist

        Liang Zhi-an, Shanghai Physiology Institute,
            otologist

        Chen Gong-bai, Department of Neurosurgery,
            Hua Shan Hospital, brain surgeon

        Wang Zheng-min, Department of Otolaryngology,
            Hua Shan Hospital.

    Unfortunately the interpreter was unfamiliar with the
technical terminology, and the discussion was held under
less than optimal conditions.  In the first part of the

discussion, Dr. Fromkin attempted to outline some of the areas in which linguists and neurosurgeons, aphasiologists, physiological psychologists, neuroanatonomists and neurophysiologists in the United States are cooperating in joint efforts to understand brain mechanisms underlying language. She discussed various experiments in dichotic listening, split-brains, the diagnosis and treatment of language disorders, and so on.  The visiting group's initial confusion as to why they were meeting with linguists (a confusion which would undoubtedly be shared by U.S. doctors under similar circumstances) was dispelled somewhat after this introduction.

Most of the discussion centered around questions raised by the Chinese group.  They were particularly interested in the split-brain experiments (commisurotomies).  They informed us that they have been conducting experiments along these lines with cats, seeking to determine information transfer between the two hemispheres.  They do not feel they are ready to perform this surgery on humans, since they believe too little is still known about possible postsurgical effects.  We were unable to provide a great deal of information on those effects, since to date no statistics have been published on the negative results of such surgical procedures.  While the Chinese appeared to be acquainted with some of the work done in the United States, particularly in Dr. Sperry's laboratory at Caltech, they sought detailed information on the experiments concerning language, spatial, temporal, etc. specializations.

They were also interested in other experiments being conducted to determine lateralization of the hemispheres, such as those using dichotic-listening and T-scope techniques.  They did not, however, indicate whether similar experiments are being conducted in the PRC.

In their split-brain experiments with cats they have found that more complex tasks show less transfer than simpler, possibly sub-cortically processed, tasks.

Dr. Liang discussed some preliminary work on the perception of tones which shows that under noise conditions, for example, telephonic communication, tones are less distorted and more intelligible then are segmental aspects of the speech signal.  He also reported on some preliminary investigations which he is carrying out concerning child language acquisition.  While he was hesitant to generalize from the scant observations made to date, he

said that the four contrasting tones are apparently acquired at an early stage, prior to the acquisition of many
segmental contrasts; moreover, the tones seem to be acquired within a very short time span.

The aphasia research similar to that done for many years
in the United States seems to be primarily concerned with
classification and diagnosis and retraining (e.g., Broca's
aphasia, receptive aphasia, agnosia, etc.). We were particularly interested in the effects of brain lesions on
the tonal aspects of Chinese, but no specific attention
has been paid to such effects. Yet impressionistically,
the Chinese specialists felt that very often tonal sub-
stitutions do not occur, even in cases of jargon aphasia
or difficulties with segmental aspects. There does not
seem to be a special discipline of speech pathology. In
the language retraining of aphasia patients, regular medical personnel work with the patients and their families.

Prior to brain surgery they administer a 'handedness
test'. For left-handers they also use, when called for,
the technique known in our country as the Wada test, that
is, the anesthetization of one or the other hemisphere by
the innoculation of sodium pentathol in the carotid ar-
teries. It was not clear whether this technique was in-
dependently developed in China or whether they adopted
its use from the reading of Western journals.

They told us that there was little joint effort with
linguists (none at all from what we could gather), but
that there was some cooperation with people working in
acoustic research, particularly as related to hearing and
perception studies. The papers, reporting on their research
findings, are published in the Journal of Chinese Medicine
and the Journal of Chinese Science. They expressed great
interest in the new journal Brain and Language and in receiving reprints on the neurolinguistic research being
conducted in the United States.

## 8. THE NATIONAL MINORITY LANGUAGES

## Introduction

The following report is based primarily on the Delegation's visit to the Central Institute for Nationalities in Peking (<u>Zhongyang Minzu Xueyuan</u>). The members of the Delegation were introduced to a number of instructors of the Institute, visited several language classes (Tibetan class for Han Chinese, Chinese grammar class for Mongol students, and Chinese classes for Kazakhs and Uighurs), toured an exhibition on the national minorities of China (history, handicrafts, paintings, national costumes, etc.), and saw the Institute's library. The more substantive part of this report is based on formal and informal discussions with the instructors at this Institute supplemented by informal discussions with Chinese linguists outside of Peking.

1. The Central Institute for Nationalities--Organization,

    Course Offerings, Cooperation with Other National

    Minority Research Institutions

This Institute was formally established in June 1951 to continue the work of the Institute for National Minorities which was set up in Yenan as early as 1941. Before the Cultural Revolution the Institute graduated 9,400 students. At present, 1,500 students are at the Institute, and more are expected to arrive soon. The present enrollment includes students from fifty-two nationalities, including Han Chinese.

The Institute is organized into five major departments:

1. Department of Cadre Training Courses

The students in this department are middle and high-

level cadres from national minority areas who study Marxism-
Leninism and the works of Chairman Mao for one year to one
and a half years.  They come from a number of autonomous
regions, autonomous counties and smaller national minority
communities.

   2.  Department of Political Science

   In this department workers, peasants, and soldiers
of different nationalities study more theoretical aspects
of Marxism-Leninism for three years.  The students in this
department are usually high school graduates (in other departments this is not necessarily so) from various national
minorities; they have at least two years of practical experience before coming to the Institute.  After graduation
they are to do theoretical work.

   3.  Department of Languages

   The main goal of this department is to train translators and interpreters for the minority languages.  The
course of study lasts three years.  Courses are offered
in Mongolian, Tibetan, Uighur, Kazakh, Korean, and a few
minor languages like Jingpo.  There are no purely linguistics courses at the Institute, but students are taught
some linguistics in the language instruction courses, for
example, phonetics.
   Before the Cultural Revolution there were specific
linguistics courses, but these have now been abolished on
the grounds that they were too theoretical in content and
too remote from the needs of language learners.  In the
future, there is a possibility that the more advanced students will be offered courses in comparative studies, for
example, comparative Turkic.
   The majority of students in this department are national minority students learning Putonghua, and taking advanced courses on the structure of their native language.
Moreover, a large number of students of Han Chinese nationality are studying Tibetan.

   4.  Department of Arts

   The goal of this department is to teach and help
develop various ethnic arts such as dancing, singing, instrumental music, handicrafts and fine arts, with the aim
of encouraging exchange of the cultures of the various
nationality areas.  After graduation the students join

theatrical performance troupes or go back to their native
regions to develop their folk arts further.

   5.  Research Department

   In this department students do research on the history and the present situation of the various national
minorities of China.

   In addition to the above-mentioned departments there
is also a Department of Preparatory Courses.  This offers
basic language and culture courses to those students who
enter the Institute without sufficient background to participate in the courses offered by the regular departments.
The students are to be prepared for entering institutions
of higher learning.

   As in other educational institutions after the Cultural
Revolution, all students devote about one-third of their
time to participation in industrial and agricultural production and military affairs outside of school.  The staff
numbers 940, including instructors, cadres, workers and
administrators.  After the Cultural Revolution, the length
of study at the Institute was reduced from four or five
years to three years or less.

   The Institute has a library of 500,000 volumes, of which
approximately 70,000 are in foreign and national minority
languages.  The library's reading room stocks newspapers
and magazines in a large variety of national minority languages.  At the time of the Delegation's visit to the library, a number of national minority language dictionaries
were on display, all of them published before the Cultural
Revolution.  The language textbooks used at the Institute
at present are all in ditto form; they are not available
outside the Institute, since major revisions are expected
in the future.  A number of textbooks and dictionaries
are in  preparation, but none have been published since
the Cultural Revolution.  However, the Institute publishes
a school journal, a biweekly bulletin, and an occasional
pamphlet, none of which were made available to the members
of the Delegation.

   National minority members participate actively in the
administration of the Institute as members of the Institute's Revolutionary Committee.  Four of the administrative
staff of seven are national minority people.

2.  Other Schools and Institutes Specializing in
    National Minority Studies

According to the members of the staff at the Central
Institute for Nationalities, there are eight institutes
or universities specializing in national minority studies.
They differ mainly in respect to the particular national
minority languages and cultures emphasized.  Specializa-
tion seems to depend on the location of the institution.
The Central Institute for Nationalities has close relations with the Kunming Institute for National Minorities,
even though there are no formal organizational ties between
them.  In the past, some graduates were exchanged, and
occasionally the two institutes cooperate on research projects.  We were told that the Kunming Institute teaches
political science, history of several national minorities
and the languages and literatures of the following nationalities: Lisu, Tai, Hani, Jingpo, Lahu and Wa.
The Central Institute for Nationalities also has very
close, though unofficial, ties with the Minority Languages
Department of the Chinese Academy of Sciences.  In 1956
the two organizations cooperated in organizing seven teams
of linguists, who did research on forty-two minority lan-
gues in sixteen separate regions.  After that research
was completed, the two organizations cooperated on the
schemes for orthographic reforms for five national minority
languages.  Some scholars hold joint appointments in the
two organizations.  The Research Institute of Nationalities
at the Academy of Sciences has two departments, one specializing in language, the other in history.  The history
department formerly was a part of the Central Institute
for Nationalities before being shifted to the Academy of
Sciences.  This shift was made because the Central Institute now emphasizes teaching, whereas the Academy emphasizes research.  Yet the Central Institute and the Department of Languages of the Research Institute of Nationalities still maintain a close relationship.
In general, it appears that the organized research and
courses on minority languages and cultures are confined
to a number of specially designated institutes and other
institutions of higher learning.  Accordingly even those
institutions of higher learning which are located in areas
with a fairly large number of national minority peoples,

but are not designated as special research and language
teaching centers for the national minorities, do not have
any national minority language courses and do not conduct
any organized research on the national minorities. To be
sure, the universities located in autonomous regions do
conduct courses in local minority languages and carry out
organized research on the local national minorities; but,
for example, Zhongshan University in Canton does not offer
any courses on the national minority languages nor conduct
any organized research on them, even though there are several national minorities in Guangdong province. Yet individual linguists may conduct their own research on national minority languages regardless of their institution-
al affiliation.

3.  General and Language Policies Affecting National

    Minorities in China

    As early as 1931, the Communist Party of China estab-
lished its policies towards national minorities: to encourage the development of all aspects of national minorities' language and culture. These policies were put into
practice in the Soviet bases located in Jiangxi province.
Later, the November 1938 session of the Central Committee
of the Chinese Communist Party discussed the problem of
national minority languages in detail. It was decided at
that time that the Party should actively help the national minorities develop their cultures and languages, both
spoken and written. In December 1947, Chairman Mao gave
a speech in which he urged that both spoken and written
languages of the national minorities be respected. These
expressions of support for the rights of the national minorities by the Chinese Communist Party were based on the
principles of Marxism-Leninism.
    After Liberation, many laws, policies, and orders re-
lating to the national minorities of China were promulgated. The 1954 Constitution has several articles dealing
with the rights of the minorities. In general, the spoken
and written languages of the national minorities are to
be respected. All national minorities have the right to
use and develop their languages. No discrimination against
national minorities and their languages is allowed. Various autonomous regions, autonomous counties (xian), and

autonomous districts (zhou) were established in areas in-
habited by national minorities. All institutions of the
state in these autonomous areas use local minority languages in their dealings with the people. The law courts
must provide the accused persons with interpreters, if
the language used in the court is not understood by the
accused. In the Xinjiang Autonomous Region, only local
languages are used as a medium of instruction in the elementary and middle schools. In the same region, the law provides that both Chinese and Uighur must be used in all public
documents. In the Mongolian Autonomous Region all documents must be in Chinese and Mongolian. Han Chinese working in these regions are required to learn the local language.
    The Nationalities Publishing House (Minzu Chubanshe)
in Peking publishes books in the five major national minority languages: Mongolian, Uighur, Tibetan, Zhuang, and
Korean. Many books, magazines, and newspapers in national
minority languages are also published by the printing
houses in the autonomous regions themselves, even in the
counties and districts. Moreover, many local newspapers
are printed in the local national minority language as
well as in Chinese.
    The Central Broadcasting Station in Peking broadcasts
in the major national minority languages; local stations
in the autonomous areas broadcast in the local minority
languages as well as in Chinese. For example, in Xinjiang
there are regular broadcasts in Chinese, Uighur, Kazakh
and Mongolian.
    Apparently, in all autonomous regions, and perhaps in
smaller autonomous units as well, the local national minority language is the medium of instruction in elementary
and middle schools; the study of Chinese begins in middle
school. Although the study of Chinese language is on a
voluntary basis, most students are reportedly eager to
learn it, in order to be able to continue with their studies at schools in the Han Chinese areas, and for the con-
venience of being able to communicate with the rest of
the people in the nation.
    In many of the elementary and middle schools visited
by the Delegation the students put on short programs including songs, dances, and acrobatics. All such performances included a few dances and songs of the national minorities of China, usually Uighur, Mongolian, Tibetan,

and Korean; the performers wore the national dress of the
minorities whose songs and dances they performed.  This
activity attests to the eagerness of the educational circles in the Han Chinese areas to make the Han majority
more aware of the culture of the national minorities.
None of the songs and dances performed, however, were
purely traditional songs and dances of national minorities,
but rather new works reflecting current political themes
and campaigns.  The songs contained at most one or two
words from national minority languages; otherwise, the
entire song was sung in Putonghua.  The same was true of
the songs and dances performed by the Song and Dance Troupe
of the Yunnan Province, whose performance the Delegation
saw in Canton.

There seem to be no special courses on the national minorities on the elementary and middle school levels in the
Han Chinese areas.  The students learn about the national
minorities in courses devoted to the history and geography
of China.

The government actively encourages the development of
the national minority languages in two important ways: language standardization and orthographic reform.  These activities are channelled through the various institutions,
but it is the government that sets up the priorities.
After a series of investigations on language variation in
several national minority areas--between 1954 and 1958
fourteen languages were investigated--, the material gathered was analyzed and choices were made as to which of the
national minority language dialects were to be designated
as the basic or standard dialects.

The principles governing reforms for national minority
languages are as follows:

a.  The ultimate goal, as for Han Chinese itself, is
the conversion of all national minority scripts to romanization.

b.  Since the system of romanizing Putonghua has already been worked out, the roman letter used to transcribe
a given sound or phoneme in a minority language should be
the same letter used to transcribe the same or a very similar sound in pinyin.

c.  Those sounds of national minority languages for
which there are no counterparts in Chinese are to be

transcribed with the existing pinyin letters with added diacritics, or by specially devised letters. In general, uniformity of romanization is desirable for all of the languages of China, but especially for related languages.

d. New loanwords from Han Chinese into national minority languages are to be transcribed according to pinyin.

e. In order to facilitate orthographic reforms in national minority languages and to promote standardization of spelling, basic dialects must be chosen as the standard languages for each national minority. This policy reflects the policy followed for Han Chinese.

The following languages, most of which did not have a written tradition, have been provided with an orthography since Liberation: Zhuang, Miao, Yi, Dong, Buyi, Li, Hani, Lisu, Wa, and Naxi. More recently, the following languages underwent orthographic reforms, that is, romanization according to the pinyin principles described above: Uighur, Kazakh, Lahu, and Jingpo.

The recently published map of China edited by the Committee on Language Reform, which uses pinyin for all place-names, adheres closely to the policies cited above, especially in the use of pinyin to transcribe native place-names in minority areas. Formerly used Chinese names for localities in national minority areas have now been replaced by the original native names. Unfortunately, the editors have omitted from the map all diacritics for Chinese tones and the special sounds found in the minority languages.

4. Identification of National Minorities--

   Theory and Practice

Members of the Delegation raised the question of what constitutes a national minority in China, since the Manchus and the Hui people are officially recognized as national minorities, in spite of the fact that Manchus are almost completely assimilated to Han Chinese in both language and custom, and the Hui people differ from Han Chinese primarily in religion. Hui people are Muslim and probably never had a separate language.

Official recognition of an ethnic group's national minority status confers certain rights and privileges on the

members of such groups.  National minority students, for
example, are given first preference for admission to institutions of higher learning, and they receive higher
stipends than Han Chinese students.  Accordingly, many
groups seek such recognition.  Members of the Central Institute for Nationalities have been called upon in the
past to aid in the nationalities identification work which
must precede official recognition of a national minority.
In this work linguists have played a very important role.

The work of identifying national minorities is still
going on.  Although fifty-four national minorities have
been officially recognized as such, presumably others have
yet to be identified.  One of the basic criteria employed
in such identification work is ethnic self-identification
of the ethnic group itself.  The members of the group are
interviewed concerning their own feelings of national identity.  Historical background also plays a role since nationalities are formed historically.

Identification of nationalities involves two basic
tasks: (1) determining whether a given community or group
is ethnically distinct from the Han Chinese majority, and
(2) whether an apparently distinct group should be identified as a distinct national minority, or considered as
part of an already recognized national minority.

The first of these tasks appears to be the more difficult one; in carrying it out, criteria other than linguistic and cultural considerations seem to be employed.  Even
though the Manchu language is probably extinct and Manchu
customs no longer differ from those of the Han Chinese,
the incontrovertible historical evidence that Manchus
were originally a separate nationality is used to back up
the feelings of self-identity felt by the Manchu people.
Similarly, the religion and many customs of the Hui people
form a sufficient basis for them to be recognized as a
separate ethnic entity, even though they employ the same
language as do the Han Chinese.  In some instances, however, where it can be proved that a certain group is
historically of Han Chinese ethnic origin, national minority status is denied.  For example, a group in Guizhou
province claimed national minority status; but upon thorough investigation they turned out to be Han Chinese who
had been influenced by the culture of the national minorities surrounding them.  Although this group differed in
customs from later Han Chinese immigrants in the province,

historically it was Han Chinese. When the group was
shown the historical evidence to this effect, it accepted
the findings and now considers itself to be Han Chinese.
    The second task is primarily assigned to linguists,
since they must identify the linguistic relationship of
a given minority language, and also the most closely related languages. Furthermore, linguists must decide
whether there are sufficient differences between a given
language and its closest relative to warrant its recognition as a separate language rather than as a dialect
of an already recognized language. After such investigations, a new national minority was recently recognized
in Tibet--the Dongba nationality. But the Xiaerba (Sherpa)
people and their language are still being investigated in
order to determine whether they form a nationality distinct
from Tibetan. As another example, the Axi people, who
live near Kunming in Yunnan province, were ascertained
to be very closely related to the Yi nationality of Sani,
even though the two groups are located fairly far from
each other. When these facts were explained to the Axi
people, they agreed that they form a part of the Yi nationality. In this way national units are identified
and consolidated.
    Several Marxist theoreticians have attempted to give
a definition of what constitutes a nationality. Stalin,
who based his ideas on Lenin's works, was of the opinion
that a group of people of the same nationality should
possess a common language, inhabit a definite geographic
region, and have common economic and cultural ties. But
it is also assumed that Marxists must analyze different
situations in order to solve particular practical problems without being too rigid in their theory. China, for
example, had long been under feudal and semi-colonial
rule, and therefore the nationalities in China have developed in very uneven, unbalanced ways. Consequently,
when one tries to apply Stalin's principles to the question of national minorities in China, one often finds
that a given Chinese ethnic group lacks one or more of
the stated characteristics of a nationality. Thus the
Hui people do not have a language distinct from Han Chinese, and only in Ningxia is there a cohesive concentration
of Hui people; in the main, Hui people are scattered all
over China. Therefore, though Stalin's principles may be
applicable to the situation in developed capitalist coun-

tries, they do not seem to be fully applicable in the Chinese context.  For this reason the Central Committee of
the Chinese Communist Party has decided that the masses
themselves be consulted for their opinions on their ethnic status.

5.  National Minority Languages of China--Current

Research and Language Reform

The languages of South and Southwestern China belong
to the Sino-Tibetan, Austroasiatic or Zhuang-Tai families.
Those of North and Northwestern China are Altaic.

5.1  Languages of South and Southwest China

Tibetan is found predominantly in Tibet; Tibetan-speaking communities are also found in Sichuan, Qinghai, Yunnan,
and Gansu.  In Tibet, all official documents are issued in
both Tibetan and Chinese, and also in certain regions of
Sichuan and Qinghai.  Moreover, the radio stations in
Tibet broadcast in Tibetan and Putonghua.  Similarly, the
Chengdu radio station in Sichuan and the Xining radio station in Qinghai also have regular Tibetan broadcasts.  The
Nationalities Publishing House in Peking publishes books
and magazines in the Tibetan language, primarily translations of Chairman Mao's works and those of Marx, Engels
and Lenin.  Local printing houses in Tibet and other regions where Tibetans live also publish newspapers, medical
books, textbooks, and so on in Tibetan.

According to radio reports, the Tibet People's Publishing House, set up during the Cultural Revolution, has put
out 1.5 million copies of books in Tibetan.  Besides books
on Marxism-Leninism, it has published such works as the
Tibetan Almanac and the Catalogue of Medicinal Herbs in
Tibet.  The circulation of the Tibet Daily, a paper established in 1956, is reported to be about 25,000.  Many films
have been dubbed in Tibetan.

Before Liberation there was only one regular primary
school in the whole of Tibet; the rest of the schooling
was available only in lamaseries and special schools for
Tibetan aristocracy.  Since Liberation, the educational
system in Tibet has expanded very rapidly.  In Lhasa alone
there are two high schools, one of which will soon be up-

graded to a university.  At the county level too, many
middle schools have been founded; and at the level of districts and communes, many elementary schools have been
established.  In the primary schools only the Tibetan language is used.  In middle schools, students begin to study
Putonghua.

A number of Han Chinese students are studying Tibetan,
and Tibetan students are studying Putonghua at the Central
Institute for Nationalities.  Since the founding of this
Institute about 200 translation workers have been trained
in Tibetan.  The Han Chinese students enrolled in the Tibetan language program come to the Institute without any
prior knowledge of Tibetan.  These students spend half a
year on mastering the rudiments of Tibetan phonetics,
phonology and syntax, and in acquiring a basic vocabulary
of 800 words.  Thereupon they and some of their teachers
are sent to Tibet for eight months, where they live and
work with the Tibetan people.  Finally the students return
to the Institute, to spend another one and a half years
perfecting their translation techniques.  In the near future, the first class of students who enrolled after the
Cultural Revolution will be graduated.  Most of the graduates will begin working as translators for the various
printing houses, especially the Nationalities Publishing
House in Peking.

At present, there is no plan to reform Tibetan orthography, but this does not mean that there will be no orthographic reform of Tibetan at some time in the future.
The present Tibetan orthography is very far removed from
the spoken language, especially the Lhasa dialect, in
which all consonant clusters have disappeared from the
spoken language, yet continue to be written.  For the
time being romanized Tibetan is used only for teaching
purposes.  Any orthographic reform of Tibetan will probably have to wait until modern standard Tibetan based on
the Lhasa dialect has been spread throughout Tibet.

In 1975 a new Chinese-Tibetan dictionary will be published by the Central Institute for Nationalities.  It
will use the traditional Tibetan orthography and spelling;
there will be no phonetic transcription of Tibetan words
since, according to the compilers, the correct pronunciation of Tibetan words can be derived from the traditional
spelling by means of regular conversion rules.  At least
some words, however, are not regular.  For the conversion

rules to work, these words will have to be respelled or
marked as exceptions in some way.  Since, however, the
dictionary is probably designed to serve the translators
of written materials rather than interpreters, these problems are not serious.  It was also reported that the 1964
edition of the <u>Han-Tibetan Dictionary</u>, a Tibetan-Tibetan
dictionary with Chinese glosses, is now being revised.

When new terminology is designed for Tibetan, many of
the social, political, and technical items are constructed
on Chinese models, though some Chinese words are borrowed
directly.  The word for 'China' currently used in Tibet
is such a direct loan from Han Chinese; the old words
<u>rgya-nag</u> and <u>rgya yul</u> are no longer used officially.  The
Tibetans also coin a small number of words, especially
where a form based on the Chinese model would either not
make sense or would have inappropriate connotations.  A
similar problem was faced earlier by Christian mission-
aries in Tibet, when they tried to translate Christian
concepts without using words which have very strong Bud-
dhist connotations for Tibetans.  In a radio report it
was claimed that some 100,000 new words and phrases have
been introduced in Tibetan since 1959.

A group of instructors at the Institute have made a
survey of Tibetan dialects and found three major dialect
groups.  The results of this survey, however, do not seem
to have been published as yet.  The Lhasa dialect is analyzed as having four tones: two basic and two derived.

Lisu, Jingpo and Lahu have relatively few speakers.
Yet by the policy of the Chinese Communist Party, the development of such languages in both their spoken and written form is to be encouraged.  In Yunnan province, where
these languages are spoken, radio stations broadcast every
day in two dialects of Lisu as well as in Jingpo and Lahu.

The Yunnan Publishing House also prints books, textbooks and newspapers in many of the local national languages.  Moreover, Jingpo is taught both at the Central
Institute for Nationalities in Peking and at the National
Minority Institute in Kunming.  A large number of translators were trained at these institutes, and many dictionaries and language textbooks have been compiled.

Other national minority languages of Southern China
are still being investigated as a preliminary to orthographic reforms, but no details concerning these languages
were given to the Delegation.  Several instructors reported

a recent discovery of a new Tibeto-Burman language called
Xifan ( 西 番 ).    This language has no tones, but has
preserved complex consonant clusters.  The investigation
of this language is still going on; so far there seem to
be no published reports on it.

5.2  Languages of North and Northwest China

    Although the greatest number of minority languages spo-
ken in Xinjiang, Inner Mongolia, and Manchuria are of the
Altaic family, two in Xinjiang belong to the Indo-European
family: Tajik and Russian.  This section will deal only
with Altaic languages.
    Uighur, a Turkic language with some 4,000,000 speakers,
is the largest and most important minority language in
North China.  It has been written since the 7th or 8th
century A.D.  Prior to the introduction of Islam in the
10th century, the Old Uighur script was employed.  After
the conversion of the Uighurs to Islam, Arabic script was
gradually adopted and has remained in use ever since.  In
the 1950's the Chinese government began to develop a Latin
script for Uighur; by 1975 this script is to replace the
Arabic script entirely.
    In the Xinjiang Uighur Autonomous Region, Uighur enjoys
equal status with Chinese in all government and party organs.  The documents of such organs are published in both
languages.  In certain autonomous districts, documents
are issued in three languages, as, for example, in the
Bayan Gool Autonomous District, where Chinese, Uighur, and
Oirat Mongolian all enjoy official status.  The Xinjiang
Ribao (Xinjiang Daily) appears in four languages: Chinese,
Uighur, Kazakh, and Oirat Mongolian.  Since Uighurs and
Kazakhs are in the process of changing to Latin script,
there are actually two editions of the paper in these two
languages, one in Arabic script and one in Latin.  Formerly the Xinjiang Ribao was also published in Sibe, a slightly reformed version of Literary Manchu; but this publication has apparently been discontinued now.  There are frequent radio broadcasts in the same four languages in which
the Xinjiang Daily is published.
    In all primary and middle schools in Uighur-speaking
areas, Uighur is used as the chief medium of instruction.
The same is true of the liberal arts departments of
Xinjiang University.  According to our hosts only Latin

script is now taught in primary and middle schools.

Uighur students in middle schools study Chinese four hours per week. Similarly, students in middle schools where Chinese is the principal language, have four hours of Uighur per week.

At present the Central Institute for Nationalities offers a course in Chinese for Uighur students. Its purpose is to train translators, who will translate Chinese materials, chiefly of an official and political nature, into Uighur. We were told that classes in Uighur for Chinese students would begin next fall. Very recently a Uighur student arrived at the Institute to learn Old Uighur. The recent discovery of hitherto-unknown texts, written in Old Uighur, necessitates the training of such specialists.

Kazakh is the second major Turkic language of Xinjiang, spoken by about a half-million people. In areas where there are significant numbers of Kazakhs, it enjoys a semi-official status. In general its fate is linked closely to that of Uighur, and its present situation very much resembles that of Uighur.

The Institute provides classes in Chinese for Kazakh students, who are chiefly being trained for translation work. We visited one such class. The teacher was explaining certain difficulties in the translation of Chinese texts; his lecture was entirely in Kazakh.

The chief of the Kazakh section at the Institute goes to the Kazakh-speaking area of Xinjiang often, and speaks Kazakh very fluently. He is also interested in Old Turkic, as well as general Turkological studies, and is well-read in Western scholarly literature. The course on Turkology, formerly offered at the Institute, has been suspended since the Cultural Revolution. It is hoped, however, that this course will resume in two to three years.

Mongolian can be roughly divided into three major dialect areas--Western, Central, and Eastern. Written Mongolian differs considerably from the contemporary dialects. Western Mongolian, spoken in Xinjiang, is often called Oirat; it has its own distinctive script. In China, Mongolian is still written in the traditional vertical script, which historically is derived from the Old Uighur script. In the 1950's, the government considered adoption of Cyrillic script, which is in use in the Mongolian People's Republic; but this idea was rejected. For the present

there seem to be no plans to reform the Mongolian script
or to change to the Latin alphabet.

In the Inner Mongolian Autonomous Region official government and party documents are issued in both Chinese
and Mongolian.  In addition to a regional daily, Mongolian-
language newspapers are also published in several administrative districts (aimag).  The Inner Mongolian Radio Station broadcasts four times daily in Mongolian.  In addition, various banners have their own radio stations which
broadcast almost exclusively in Mongolian.

Since the early fifties there has been very extensive
publication in Mongolian.  Over 2,700 titles and 17,680,000
volumes have appeared during this period.  It was not clear
whether these figures include primary and secondary school
texts.

Starting in 1953, an extensive survey of Mongolian dialects was initiated in Inner Mongolia and other areas where
Mongolian is spoken.  The material from this survey has
been used in standardization work; very little of it has
been published so far.

Four new dictionaries are in the process of completion.
A new Chinese-Mongolian dictionary is being prepared by
the Mongolian Linguistic and Cultural Institute; the Nationalities Publishing House in Peking is also working on
a new Chinese-Mongolian dictionary.  The Inner Mongolian
University is responsible for compiling a Mongolian-Chi-
nese dictionary, and the Inner Mongolian Normal College
is working on a monolingual Mongolian dictionary.

We visited a class in Chinese translation for Mongols.
The teacher was lecturing in Mongolian on Chinese modifiers
(čimeg üge).

Sibe is a dialect of Manchu, spoken by about 20,000
people in the Ili region of Xinjiang.  For the written language a slightly reformed version of Literary Manchu is
used.  A newspaper called the Xinlu Bao (The New Road) is
published in Xingiang.  A number of Sibe are working on
Manchu documentary material in the Imperial Palace in
Peking.  Sibe has been taught only once at the Central
Institute, and there are no plans to offer it at any time
in the future.

Korean is spoken by a sizable minority in the North-
eastern provinces.  Yet forty-six percent of all Koreans
in China, 540,000 people, live in the Yanbian Korean Autonomous District along the Tumen river.

The Koreans of China use the same written language as that employed in North Korea. Although the use of their language was prohibited during the Japanese occupation and before Liberation, the Koreans of China now have the right to use it in both official and private life.

In 1952 primary education became universal throughout the district; lower middle school education was set up soon afterwards. In 1949 one university was established in the district. In 1958, a medical and an agricultural college were set up. Extramural education programs are well-developed.

A broadcasting station in the district broadcasts regularly in Korean. Moreover, a Korean newspaper, Yanbian Ribao, is published in the district. There are two publishing houses: Education Publishing House and People's Publishing House. Finally, a group was established in 1957 to carry out language reforms and oversee general language development.

In addition to the languages mentioned above, numerous other Altaic languages are spoken in China. None of them has a written form to our knowledge. We were not given any specific information concerning them during any of our contacts with the members of the Institute.

## 5.3 Comparative Studies

A number of scholars expressed deep interest in comparative studies concerning genetic relationships between national minority languages spoken in China and language groups outside of China. These scholars appeared to be current in their knowledge of foreign literature in this field and eager to receive publications from foreign scholars. They must, however, concentrate their attention on language teaching, particularly the training of interpreters for national minority languages, on language standardization, and on orthographic reforms. Therefore any historical/comparative research on the national minority languages will most likely be done only to the extent it enhances the achievement of the above-mentioned practical goals.

At present very few books written in minority languages are available for purchase abroad, with the exception of translations of political materials and a pictorial magazine, Minzu Huabao; this is published in Han Chinese,

Uighur, Kazakh, Mongolian, Korean, Tibetan, and Zhuang.
According to the information given us, acquisition of other publications in minority languages, especially textbooks and local newspapers, would require a high-level
government decision.

# 9. LANGUAGE THEORY IN THE PEOPLE'S REPUBLIC OF CHINA

## Introduction

Since the Cultural Revolution, linguistics, like all other disciplines, has had one major focus: "to serve prolatarian politics." Research on the nature and structure of language as a goal in itself is not being pursued. There are no linguistic courses, nor departments of linguistics. Instead, linguistics is integrated into other courses. But this so-called integration consists mainly of the use of grammatical or phonetic explanations in language classes. Even the extent of explicit syntactic and phonological statements has been considerably reduced. The "integration of linguistics" does not in any way mean, therefore, that students study the nature of language, or linguistic theory. Teaching and research devoted to pure linguistics is opposed on the grounds that theory must be combined with practice, and that practice takes precedence.

All linguistic work, as far as we could ascertain, is therefore directed at those areas which have immediate practical and political applications: the teaching of Chinese and national minority languages; the teaching of foreign languages; language reform, including the popularization of Putonghua and pinyin, and the simplification of characters; to a lesser extent, dialect surveys and dialect analyses, largely for contrasts with Putonghua as part of the language reform program; the use of phonetics for the above and for the teaching of the deaf; the decipherment of ancient texts and the study of ancient Chinese as part of the movement to criticize Lin Piao and Confucius; orthographic reform and the establishment of phonemically-based romanized alphabets for national minority languages.

This approach to the study of language was summarized for us, and referred to by a number of linguists in the

course of our visit.  We were told, however, that the emphasis on practice does not imply a negation of the importance of theory, but that theory must be a guide to
practice and arises from practice.  It was also acknowledged that research in mathematics, and in the physical
and biological sciences may lead to theoretical developments which may not immediately have practical applications, but possible future uses.  Thus, although the major
research efforts are currently directed toward agriculture
and economics, pure research is conducted in some areas,
the extent determined by the overall scientific plan.
But very little linguistics research seems to be included
in the present plan.

The practical work of linguists is guided by the Marxist-
Leninist Theory of Language.  This dialectical-materialist
approach to language is based on the writings of Marx,
Engels, Lenin, and, in particular, Stalin.  Stalin's statements on language, first published in Pravda in 1950, appeared in the midst of a debate in Soviet linguistic circles concerning the linguistic theory of N. Y. Marr, whose
views, due to Stalin's intervention, were at the time pronounced anti-Marxist.  Stalin's statements are widely
available in the PRC, as in the English publication entitled: Marxism and the Problems of Linguistics, by J. V.
Stalin; Peking: Foreign Language Press, 1972.  In what
follows, all of the citations refer to this publication
unless otherwise indicated.

We were also told that "foreign linguists" such as
Jespersen and Bloomfield are read (and even Chomsky, but
not as yet in any thorough way) in keeping with the dic-
tum "to make the past serve the present and foreign things
serve China."  As far as we were able to learn, however,
Stalin's position on the nature of language, on standard
languages and on historical change, and on the relationship between language and thought represents the accepted
theory of linguistics in the PRC.  In the summary of these
views which follows, there is no attempt to comment on the
individual points critically.  We are only concerned with
reporting the linguistic activities in the PRC as they
became known to us.

Some of the views held in the PRC would obviously be
supported by a wide group of non-Marxist linguists.  Others
are being debated in the Western world.  Still others would

be considered outside the scope of linguistic theory.
Whatever the position of linguists elsewhere, for an understanding of current theoretical and practical linguistic activities in the PRC, it is essential to know the
views on language which are referred to as Marxist-Leninist
Theory. These are presented briefly under the various
topics treated in this chapter.

## 1.  Linguistics as a Science

Although language is considered primarily a social
phenomenon, it possesses specific features which distinguish it from all other phenomena: it serves society as
a means of communication, it enables social production
and cooperative efforts in politics, culture, social and
everyday life, it is the means for "exchanging thought."
Because of these unique features language is considered
to be "the object of study by an independent science--lin-
guistics." (p.34)
At the present time in the PRC we saw no indication that
this view was considered important, if an independent
science would entail a body of scholars developing theory
as well as applying that theory.  Nor did we find any debate or discussion on the theory which is being applied,
despite the fact that the pamphlet which summarizes the
view on linguistics in the PRC also states that "no science
can develop and flourish without a battle of opinions,
without freedom of criticism." (p.29)  Instead, linguistics is directed at social problems; the linguistics we
found might be more precisely named socio-linguistics,
or even applied linguistics.

## 2.  Language as a Social Phenomenon

According to Marxist-Leninist theory, language is not
the product of any particular economic structure or class,
it is not part of the 'superstructure' of society, but is
rather a product of the "whole course of history of the
society...created by all the classes." (p.5)  It has as
its main function the communication between all classes
of any society.  Therefore when the economic base is
changed, and when other changes occur, even revolutionary
changes, there is no necessity for the creation of a new

language; the basic structure of the language remains in-
tact.

Language is intimately connected with man's productive
activity. Without language, men could not communicate
their thoughts, nor could they participate in productive
labor. "Without a language understood by a society and
common to all its members, that society must cease to
produce, must disintegrate and cease to exist...In this
sense,...while it is a medium of intercourse, it is at the
same time an instrument of struggle and development of society." (p.21, our emphasis)

This view is clearly reflected in the language reform
movement for the popularization of Putonghua. A common
language is considered a necessity for communication between all the people of China, and for the "construction
of a socialist society." The movement to popularize
Putonghua and pinyin is thus a direct application of this
theoretical position.

3.  Language Structure

The works of Engels, Lenin, and Stalin contain very
little on the internal structure of language. Stalin
discusses this question very superficially, not going beyond the statement that a language consists of both the
vocabulary, as the basic building blocks, and the grammar
(morphology, syntax), which consists of the rules for the
formation of words and sentences. He also notes that
grammatical rules are abstract in the sense that they refer "to all sentences in general, irrespective of the con-
crete form of any sentence in particular."

Although Stalin did not discuss phonology, clearly the
work in contrastive analysis and the phonological descriptions used in language teaching are based on some phonological theory. Yet little phonetic research is being carried
on; the phonetics utilized in classes is that of English
phoneticians like Daniel Jones. That is, transcription
is taught, and articulatory descriptions are provided.
Nor is there interest in syntactic theory. Further, although according to Stalin "semantics (semasiology) is
one of the important branches of linguistics" and "the
semantic aspect of words and expressions is of serious
importance in the study of language," the only interest

in this sphere of linguistics which we observed was in the
lexicography work concerned with changes in meanings of
words and in definitions of newly created words.
    Whatever knowledge of the phonology, syntax, and seman-
tics of Chinese is utilized then, appears to be based on
past descriptive and theoretical work.  No new specialists
are being trained in these areas.  But students are given
information to collect the pronunciation of word lists,
or to prepare new teaching materials, as indicated in
Chapter 7, Section 1.b.  It is of course possible that
this is not the whole picture, but our discussions throughout our visit led us to this conclusion.

## 4.  Language Development and Change

    The origin of language is traced back to the very be-
ginning of society.  Language arose, according to this
view, with the development of productive labor.  But in
its earliest stages, before there were social classes, it
existed as a very simple system "with a very meager stock
of words, but with a grammatical system of its own," (p.25)
primitive though it was.  With the emergence of classes,
of writing and literature, and with the rise of nations,
of the state and of trade, great changes occurred.  Such
changes are equated with language improvement.
    Language is in a constant state of change, though the
changes are neither revolutionary nor qualitative.  The
vocabulary, most reflective of changes in society, changes
most rapidly; new words enter the language, obsolete words
disappear, semantic change occurs.  The syntax changes
more slowly but "becomes more perfected, improves its
rules, makes them more specific and acquires new rules."
    Where two languages come into conflict or are "crossed,"
no new third language emerges; rather, the basic grammatical structure of one persists, usually the language of
the conquerors, enriched by the vocabulary of the con-
quered.  Because of the importance of social influences
"language and its development can only be studied in con-
nection with the history and development of society and
the people who are its creators and repositories." (p.20)
    Among other aims, the "comparative-historical method"
and the attempts to establish genetic groupings of related
languages are accordingly valuable "to linguistics and

the study of the laws of language development." (p.32)
    These views on language development are reflected to
some degree in the work of the lexicographers and the investigation of the languages of the national minorities.
Moreover, the historical investigation of languages is
applied in the identification of minorities.  It is also
important in the understanding of important texts of the
past, such as those of Confucius and the Legalists, which,
as noted above, are now being widely studied and discussed,
as contemporary ideology is scrutinized and formulated.
    The new dictionaries being prepared are concerned with
the redefinition of old words as a reflection of the social
changes which have occurred, as well as the collection of
new words "created by the masses" in the various struggles
after Liberation.  For dictionaries are "instruments of
struggle," the new definitions being viewed, we imagine,
in keeping with Chairman Mao's statement that in the fight
against the counterrevolutionary class "it is always necessary first of all to create public opinion, to do work
in the ideological sphere" (Yang Rong-guo: 'The Struggle
of Materialism Against Idealist Apriorism During the Western and Eastern Han Dynasties' in Selected Articles Criticizing Lin Piao and Confucius, Foreign Language Press;
Peking, 1974).
    In the effort to determine, what is or is not a national
minority in the PRC, the people's language and their past
is investigated in relation to the history of both.  As
indicated above, the definition of minorities has been a
difficult problem.  One means to a solution of the problem has been historical and comparative linguistics.

5.  Dialects, "Jargons" and Local Languages

    In keeping with the view that there is no such thing
as a class language, the "dialects" and "jargons" created
by the ruling class are considered "offshoots of the common national language, devoid of all linguistic independ-
ence and doomed to stagnation." (p.12)
    Before the development of unified nations there could
be no common language due to the separation of tribes and
nationalities, each with its own form of speech.  Some
local "territorial" dialects remain and, distinct from
"class dialects" which are used by "a narrow social upper

crust..., serve the mass of the people and have a grammatical system and basic word stock of their own." These
local dialects "may become the basis of national languages
and develop into independent national languages." (p.41)
    This approach to territorial dialects and the language
of national minorities is seen in the work of linguists
on dialect studies and in the descriptive work on the non-
Han languages. While the immediate dying-out of local languages is not foreseen, the long-range view seems to be
that expressed by Stalin: "After victory of socialism on
a world scale...as a result of a prolonged economic, political and cultural cooperation of nations, there will
first appear most enriched unified zonal languages, and
subsequently the zonal languages will merge into a single
international language." (pp.51-52) It is not clear, however, whether the Chinese foresee one united Chinese language before the emergence of "socialism on a world scale."
The current efforts in favor of a common language and a
simplified writing system, which have occupied much of
this report, then reflect the theoretical position on the
importance of one central language for a modern state.

## 6. Language and Thought

    Language is viewed as "an instrument (to)...exchange
thoughts, (and is)...directly connected with thinking."
(p.20) Marx and Engels define language as "the immediate
reality of thought," as "practical,...actual consciousness."
(p.35) "Ideas," Marx says, "do not exist divorced from
language."
    The Chinese view on the acquisition of language, like
the acquisition of all knowledge, is basically an empiri-
cist one. According to Lenin (as quoted in "Three Major
Struggles on China's Philosophical Front," Peking): "Not
only is the transition from matter to consciousness dialectical, but also that from sensation to thought." In
the same pamphlet the view is expressed that it is only
through repeated practice that "people can advance from
ignorance to knowledge and from incomplete knowledge to
relatively complete knowledge." This view of the priority
of "perceptual knowledge" is related to the sharp opposition against the Confucian notion of "a priori knowledge."
While the criticism of innate a priori knowledge is not

specifically referenced to language, it would hold for
language learning.
     This theoretical position strongly influences the meth-
ods we observed in the teaching of foreign languages:
words, phrases, and sentences must be learned through
practice first.   Then the "perceptual knowledge can lead
to the formation of generalizations."  Yet a difference
between first and second language learning is recognized,
since children, through practice alone, through perceptual
knowledge, are capable of abstracting the general rules.
Adults, on the other hand, require that some of the rules
be provided, after the necessary practice.
     The view that "thoughts arise in the mind of man prior
to their being expressed in speech" is opposed since "Bare
thoughts, free of the linguistic material, free of the
'natural matter' of language do not exist." (p.37) Language, and therefore thought, is equated with speech.
But this position is contradicted, since although "deaf-
mutes are deprived of the faculty of speech (and) their
thoughts cannot arise on the basis of linguistic material"
they can think; their thoughts arise "on the basis of the
images, sensations and conceptions," which relate to objects
in the real world and are sensed through the organs of
sensation (p.45).   It is not clear how "deaf-mutes, who
have no language at their disposal and whose thoughts,
of course, cannot arise on the basis of linguistic material"
can then think on the basis of non-linguistic images.  Yet
the Chinese can hardly accept this view completely regard-
ing the deaf, since, as noted in Chapter 7, in addition
to the attempt to the spoken language, sign-language is
used.
     Thought and language, according to F. Engels (Anti-
Duhring, New York: International Publishers; 1935, p.35)
are not only reflections of the perceived world, but also
"products of the human brain...The material, sensuously
perceptible world to which we ourselves belong is the only reality...Our consciousness and thinking, however supra-
sensuous they may seem, are the product of a material,
bodily organ, the brain."  There is no discussion of such
a "materialist" approach in Stalin.  Nor did we hear any
discussion on the brain mechanisms underlying language.
Given that language is the "material embodiment of thinking"
which is a product of the brain, one might expect some

interest in what is now called neurolinguistics.  But the
view of language as a social phenomenon, and the particular
political purpose which this view supports, clearly far
outweigh or completely drown any interest in the mental
aspects of language.

As this report suggests throughout, linguistics is practiced for its social utility.  Any sphere of linguistics
which does not seem to have immediately practical ends at
present is put in abeyance.  In the foreseeable future
then advances in theoretical linguistics, in psycho- and
neurolinguistics, in typology and historical linguistics
will have to be sought elsewhere.  But linguists elsewhere can look to their colleagues in China for remarkable
achievements in the standardization of Putonghua, in the
development of a simplified writing system, and in the
effective teaching of minority languages and foreign languages, as well as Putonghua.

# APPENDIX I


## ITINERARY OF THE DELEGATION

October 16 - November 13, 1974

### Wednesday, October 16

P.M.      Arrival in Peking via JAL from Tokyo
          Brief tour of nearby sites by car

Evening:  Welcoming banquet at the Peking Duck Restau-
          rant, hosted by Xu Yun-bei, Vice-Chairman of
          the Peking Revolutionary Committee and Respon-
          sible Person of the Capital Educational Cir-
          cles.

### Thursday, October 17

A.M.      Peking Language Institute

P.M.          "         "          "

Evening:  Continued discussions at PLI

### Friday, October 18

A.M.      No. 15 Middle School

P.M.      Summer Palace

Evening:  Movie: The Shining Red Star

## Saturday, October 19

| | |
|---|---|
| A.M. | Temple of Heaven |
| | Shopping at the Friendship Store and on Wang Fu-jing |
| P.M. | Shuang Qiao People's Commune |
| Evening: | Circus at the Workers' Gymnasium |

## Sunday, October 20

The Great Wall and the Ming Tombs

## Monday, October 21

| | |
|---|---|
| A.M. | Central Institute for Nationalities |
| P.M. | "          "          "          " |
| Evening: | Visit to hotel by professors from Peking Language Institute |

## Tuesday, October 22

| | |
|---|---|
| A.M. | Imperial Palace and museum |
| P.M. | Fu Sui Jing Street Committee, West City District |
| Evening: | Visit to hotel by lexicographers |

## Wednesday, October 23

| | |
|---|---|
| A.M. | Peking University |
| P.M. | "          " |
| Evening: | Visit to hotel by professors from the Central Institute for Nationalities |

Thursday, October 24

    A.M.       Third School for the Deaf (Group A)

                Imperial Palace Museum (Group B)

    P.M.       Visit to hotel by the Committee on Chinese
                Language Reform

    Evening:  Free

Friday, October 25

    A.M.       Printing Press (Group A)

                Shopping (Group B)

    Luncheon: Visit to hotel by Marcelina Ye, U.S.
                citizen teaching English at Peking
                University

    P.M.       Shopping on Liu li chang

    Evening:  Reception at U.S. Liaison Office and
                banquet for Peking linguists, hosted
                by the American Delegation at the Cheng
                du Restaurant

Saturday, October 26

    A.M.       Six-hour train ride to Anyang

    P.M.       Visit to Anyang Archaeological Station,
                before driving to Linxian

    Evening:  Free

Sunday, October 27

    A.M.       Visit to the Red Flag Canal

    P.M.       "    "      "     "

    Evening:  Banquet

Itinerary of the Delegation

## Monday, October 28

A.M.      Machine-building factory and production
          brigade

P.M.      Car ride to Anyang and train to Zhengzhou

Evening:  Banquet hosted by Wang Xi-zhang, Director
          of the Henan Provincial Bureau of Education

## Tuesday, October 29

A.M.      Wei Er Lu Primary School, Zhengzhou

P.M.      Yellow River Exhibit and car ride to the
          Yellow River; Henan Provincial Museum

Evening:  Song and dance performance and acrobatics
          by primary and middle school students,
          given at No. 7 Middle School

## Wednesday, October 30

A.M.      No. 7 Middle School

P.M.      Travel by plane to Sian

          Visit to Da Yan Pagoda and Banpo neolithic
          village

Evening:  Banquet hosted by Wen Jian-bai, Leading
          Member of the Provincial Education Bureau

## Thursday, October 31

A.M.      Shaanxi Normal College

P.M.      Travel to Yenan by plane

Evening:  Free

Friday, November 1

> A.M.       Museum of the Revolution
>            The Yenan pagoda
>
> P.M.       Former residences of Chairman Mao
>            Site of the Seventh National Congress of
>            the CCP
>            Zao Yuan (Chairman's former residence and
>            meeting hall of the CCPCC)
>
> Evening:   Banquet hosted by Zhang Mao yuan, Deputy
>            Director of the Yenan District Bureau of
>            Education
>            Movie at the hotel: A Story of the Court
>                                Facing the Sun

Saturday, November 2

> A.M.       The headquarters of the Eighth Route Army
>            at Wang Jia ping
>
> P.M.       Return to Sian by plane
>            Hua Qing Chi villa and hot springs
>
> Evening:   Movie at the hotel: Azalea Mountain

Sunday, November 3

> A.M.       Shaanxi Provincial Museum
>            Handicrafts factory
>
> P.M.       Travel by plane to Shanghai
>
> Evening:   Free

Monday, November 4

> A.M.       Cao Yang First Primary School
>
> P.M.       Fudan University

Evening:  Acrobatics performance

## Tuesday, November 5

A.M.        Shanghai Industrial Exhibit
            Shanghai Municipal Museum
            Shopping at the Friendship Store

P.M.        Children's Palace (Group A)
            Deaf-Mute School (Group B)

Evening:  Banquet hosted by Zou Jian qiu, Responsible
            Person, Revolutionary Committee of the
            Shanghai Municipal Bureau of Education

## Wednesday, November 6

A.M.        Train ride to Hangzhou

P.M.        Liu He Pagoda
            Tiger Spring
            Chrysanthemum exhibit

Evening:  Train ride to Suzhou, via Shanghai

## Thursday, November 7

A.M.        Garden of the Master of the Nets (Wang
            Shi Yuan)
            Sandalwood fan factory
            Garden of the Forest of the Lion (Shizi
            Lin)
            Garden of the Humble Administrator (Zhuo Zheng
            Shopping at the Friendship Store    Yuan)
            Xuan Miao Guan

Luncheon: Banquet hosted by Zhang Yu-ju of the Suzhou
            Bureau of Education

P.M.        Embroidery factory
            Tiger Hill
            Return to Shanghai by train

Evening:  Visit to hotel by Shanghai neurologists

## Friday, November 8

A.M.        Shanghai Normal College

P.M.        Shanghai Foreign Language Institute

Evening:  Visit to hotel by Fudan University professors
          and students

## Saturday, November 9

A.M.        Fan Gua Lane Committee

P.M.        Travel to Canton by plane
            Canton Trade Fair

Evening:  Banquet at Friendship Restaurant

## Sunday, November 10

A.M.        Drive to Fo Shan
            Ancestral Temple (Zu Miao)
            Shi Wan pottery factory

Luncheon: Overseas Hotel

P.M.        Paper-cutting factory
            Drive back to Canton
            No. 61 Middle School

Evening:  Song and dance performance at Friendship
          Theater

Monday, November 11

A.M.        Zhongshan University

P.M.        The Mosque (Huai Sheng Si)

            Pavilion Overlooking the Sea (Zhen Hai Lou),
            now the Guangzhou Museum

            Peasant Movement Institute

Evening:    Free

Tuesday, November 12

A.M.        Return to Peking by plane

P.M.        Free

Evening:    Farewell banquet hosted by the Americans
            at the Xiang Jiang Restaurant

Wednesday, November 13

A.M.        Final discussions with escorts on future
            prospects for linguistic exchanges (Chairman,
            Secretary, and Sollenberger)

            Visit by Lü Bi-song and Mao Cheng-dong from
            Peking Language Institute

            Visit to air-raid shelter

P.M.        Departure for Tokyo via JAL

# APPENDIX II

## LISTS OF OUR HOSTS, OUR ESCORTS,
## AND OF SPECIALISTS WHOM WE MET

(Chinese characters are included
when they have been verified.)

Peking          October 16 - 26, 1974

Hosts:          Peking Educational Circles

徐运北          Xu Yun-bei

Vice-Chairman, Peking Revolutionary
Committee; Responsible Person, Capital
Educational Circle

韓作黎          Han Zuo-li

Responsible Person, Peking Education
Bureau; Responsible Person, Capital
Educational Circle

胡守鑫          Hu Shou-xin

Responsible Person, Foreign Relations
Section, Science and Education Group,
State Council; Responsible Person,
Capital Educational Circle

Delegation's Escorts

李顺兴          Li Shun-xing

Official, Foreign Relations Section,
Science and Education Group, State Council

毛 国 华    Mao Guo-hua

Staff Member, Chinese People's Association for Friendship with Foreign Countries

陈 久 长    Chen Jiu-chang

Official, Science and Education Group, State Council

戚　　诛    Qi Yong

Teacher, Peking Language Institute

吴 淑 洁    Wu Shu-jie

Official, Science and Education Group, State Council

## Peking Language Institute 北 京 语 言 学 院

This Institute was founded in 1962, having previously functioned as the foreign students' department of Peking University. Its purpose is twofold: to provide one year's preparation in Chinese for foreign students, who will go on to study their specialties at other institutions, and to teach foreign languages to Chinese students. The Institute also provides post-graduate training for language cadres.

There are three departments: 1) the First Foreign Students Department, 2) the Second Foreign Students Department, and 3) the Foreign Language Department for Chinese students. Elementary Chinese is taught in the first two departments; in the third department, Spanish, Japanese, English, Arabic, French, German, and Russian are taught.

The enrollment of foreign students is currently 370, from forty countries. The 1975 enrollment is expected to increase considerably.

苏　　林    Su Lin

Chief Responsible Person, Peking Language Institute

王　　文　Wang Wen
　　　　　Responsible Person, Peking Language
　　　　　Institute

吳　　塘　Wu Tang
　　　　　Responsible Person, Peking Language
　　　　　Institute

唐　騰　义　Tang Teng-yi
　　　　　Responsible Person, Foreign Relations
　　　　　Group

张　延　令　Zhang Yan-ling
　　　　　Responsible Person, Education Revolution
　　　　　Group

吕　必　松　Lü Bi-song
　　　　　Leader, First Foreign Language Depart-
　　　　　ment

毛　成　栋　Mao Cheng-dong
　　　　　Teacher of Chinese

赵　淑　集　Zhao Shu-hua
　　　　　Teacher of Chinese

刘　　泃　Liu Xun
　　　　　Teacher of Chinese

程　美　珍　Cheng Mei-zhen
　　　　　Teacher of Chinese

吴　叔　平　Wu Shu-ping
　　　　　Teacher of Chinese

钟　　樱　Zhong Qin
　　　　　Teacher of Chinese

许 才 德.    Xu Cai-de
          Teacher of English
          (Interpreter)

Friday, October 18

Peking No. 15 Middle School   北京第十五中学

   No. 15 Middle School, founded in 1952, currently enrolls
2,200 students in forty-one classes.  There are 160 teachers
and staff members.  The length of schooling is five years,
including both junior and senior middle school.
   The subjects taught are politics, Chinese, mathematics,
foreign languages (thirty-nine classes learn English and
two learn Russian), physics, chemistry, history, geography,
basic agriculture, physical education, music, and fine arts.

李 顺 发    Li Shun-fa
          Vice-Chairman of Revolutionary
          Committee

苏 瑞 珍    Su Rui-zhen
          Member, Revolutionary Committee

Saturday, October 19

Shuang Qiao People's Commune  双桥人民公社

庄 和 善    Zhuang He-shan
          Vice-Chairman of Revolutionary
          Committee

Monday, October 21

Central Institute for Nationalities  中央民族学院

   In 1950 and 1951, eleven institutes for nationalities
were set up; the Central Institute was founded in June
1951 (see Chapter 8).  There are six departments (see
Chapter 8, Section 1):

   1)  Department of Cadre Training Courses

2) Department of Political Science
3) Department of Languages
4) Department of Arts
5) Research Department
6) Department of Preparatory Courses

宗　　群　　Zong Qun
　　　　　　Vice-Chairman, Revolutionary
　　　　　　Committee

札　　西　　Zha Xi
　　　　　　Vice-Chairman, Revolutionary
　　　　　　Committee (Tibetan)

张 寿 泉　　Zhang Shou-quan
　　　　　　Chief, Administrative Office

费 孝 通　　Fei Xiao-tong
　　　　　　Professor in Research Department

马 学 良　　Ma Xue-liang
　　　　　　Professor, Department of Languages

于 道 泉　　Yu Dao-quan
　　　　　　Professor, Department of Languages

何　　润　　He Run
　　　　　　Teacher, Cadre Training Division
　　　　　　(Bai nationality, Yunnan)

哈 未 提　　Ha-Wei-ti (Hamid Tümür)
　　　　　　Teacher, Department of Languages
　　　　　　(Uighur)

田 中 山　　Tian Zhong-shan
　　　　　　Teacher, Department of Languages
　　　　　　(Gao Shan, Taiwan)

戴 庆 厦　Dai Qing-xia
Teacher, Department of Languages

洛 桑 贡 嘎　Luo-Sang Gong-ga
Teacher, Department of Languages
(Tibetan)

金 道 权　Jin Dao-quan
Teacher, Department of Languages
(Korean)

罗 秉 芬　Luo Bing-fen
Teacher, Department of Languages

松 儒 布　Song Ru-bu
Teacher, Department of Languages
(Mongolian)

覃 克 骏　Chin Ke-jun
Office Cadre (Zhuang)

苏 儒 光　Su Ru guang
Cadre of Research Department (Li)

拉 斯 格 蚂　La-si Ge-ma
Student, Language and Literature
Department (Mongolian)

韓 古 丽　Han Gu li
Student, Language and Literature
Department (Uighur)

玉 素 甫　Yu Su-fu
Student, Language and Literature
Department (Kazakh)

索 朗 卓 嘎　Suo-lang Zhuo-ga
Student, Language and Literature
Department (Tibetan)

方 伯 龙    Fang Bo long
            Teacher, Language Department

            Geng Shih-min
            Teacher, Language Department
            (Kazakh)

Tuesday, October 22

Fu Sui Jing Street Committee, West City District

福 绥 境 街 道 委 员 会

Lexicographers (evening)

王 维 新    Wang Wei-xin
            Peking Language Institute

曹 乃 木    Cao Nai-mu
            First Normal School

潘 逊 皓    Pan Xun-hao
            No. 2 Middle School

Wednesday, October 23

Peking University 北 京 大 学

    Established in 1898, the university has been a leading
center of learning and of revolutionary change. There are
currently twenty faculties--seven liberal arts departments,
ten natural sciences departments, and three language de-
partments--with seventy-five specialties. Since the Cultural Revolution 7,600 students have been enrolled, and
the first two classes have graduated. Now there are about
5,000 undergraduate students and 900 graduate students.
The university aims to have 10,000 students in the future.
At the present time 180 foreign students from twenty-five
countries are enrolled. The faculty numbers 2,600.
    Students spend one-third of their time in factories,

shops, or communes, implementing the policy of combining theory with practice. The university runs seven factories and twenty-seven workshops, and has working relationships with sixty-five factories outside the university.

周 培 源　Zhou Pei-yuan
Vice-Chairman, Revolutionary Committee

倪 孟 雄　Ni Meng-xiong
Responsible Person, Office of Revolutionary Committee

袁 家 骅　Yuan Jia-hua
Professor, Department of Chinese

朱 德 熙　Zhu De-xi
Professor, Department of Chinese

孙 亦 骊　Sun Yi-li
Responsible Person, English Division, Department of Western Languages

郭 锡 良　Guo Xi-liang
Teacher, Department of Chinese

王 福 堂　Wang Fu-tang
Teacher, Department of Chinese

徐 同 锵　Xu Tong-qiang
Teacher, Department of Chinese

李 应 久　Li Ying-jiu
Cadre, Office of Revolutionary Committee

岑 麒 祥　Cen Qi-xiang
Professor, Department of Chinese

Thursday, October 24

<u>Committee on Chinese Language Reform</u> 文字改革委员会

叶 赖 士    Ye Lai-shi
          Responsible Person

陈 乃 华    Chen Nai-hua
          Research Worker

曹 澄 方    Cao Cheng-fang
          Research Worker (Putonghua)

孙   坚    Sun Jian
          Research Worker (character reform)

Saturday, October 26

<u>Anyang</u> (Train Station)

          Yan Zhe
          Leading Member, Anyang Education
          Bureau

          Wang An-shan
          Leading Member, Foreign Affairs Group,
          Anyang Administrative Region

          Wang Ya-zhi
          Staff Member, Foreign Affairs Group

          Yan
          Staff Member, Foreign Affairs Group

          Feng
          Staff Member, Foreign Affairs Group

## Linxian        October 26 - 28

曹 龙 衣     Cao Long-yi

Director, Linxian Bureau of Culture
and Education

郭 太 福     Guo Tai-fu

Responsible Person, Linxian Office of
Foreign Affairs

秦 永 昌     Qin Yong-chang

Staff Member, Linxian Office of Foreign
Affairs

## Zhengzhou    October 29 - 30

王 锡 章     Wang Xi-zhang

Director, Henan Provincial Bureau of
Education

吕 兆 明     Lü Zhao-ming

Responsible Person, Henan Provincial
Office of Foreign Affairs

葛 玉 怀     Ge Yu-huai

Director, Zhengzhou Bureau of Education

赵   仁     Zhao Ren

Responsible Person, Zhengzhou Office of
Foreign Affairs

尤 滋 洲     Yu Zi-zhou

Official, Henan Provincial Office of
Foreign Affairs

李 联 章     Li Lian-zhang

Staff Member, Zhengzhou Office of
Foreign Affairs

陈 国 彦
Chen Guo-yan
Staff Member, Zhengzhou Bureau of
Education

李 建 修
Li Jian-xiu
Staff Member, Zhengzhou Bureau of
Education

October 29

Wei Er Lu Primary School ("Second Horizontal Road")

纬 二 路 小 学

Yao Zhi-ping
Chairman of Revolutionary Committee

Zhang Ai-fang
Leading Member of educational district

Fu
Leader of workers' propaganda team

October 30

No. 7 High School

Zhang
Chairman of Revolutionary Committee

Ding Yan
Vice-Chairman, Revolutionary Committee

Zhang Huan-ying
Vice-Chairman, Revolutionary Committee

Hui Yi-tian
Vice-Chairman, Revolutionary Committee

Xu Ming
Vice-Chairman, Revolutionary Committee

<u>Sian</u>            October 30 - 31, November 2 - 3

温 钊 白     Wen Jian-bai
Leading Member, Provincial Education
Bureau; Responsible Person, Provincial
Educational Circles

孙         Sun Yi
Director, Provincial Foreign Affairs
Group

高 济 安     Gao Ji-an
Director, Administrative Office of
Provincial Education Bureau

王 保 民     Wang Bao-min
Staff, Provincial Foreign Affairs Group

范 子 保     Fan Zi-bao
Staff, Provincial Foreign Affairs Group

何 克 敬     He Ke-jing
Staff, Provincial Foreign Affairs Group
(Interpreter)

October 31

<u>Shaanxi Normal College</u> 陕西师范学院

The main task of Shaanxi Normal College, founded in
1952, is to train teachers for middle schools. After the
Cultural Revolution enrollment resumed in 1972 and there
are currently 2,000 students in ten departments. The five
liberal arts departments include politics, education, Chinese language, foreign languages (English and Russian),
and history; the five natural sciences departments include
mathematics, physics, chemistry, biology, and geography.

There are 1,100 teachers and staff members. The library
contains 900,000 volumes.
   The science departments have permanent links with sixty-
nine factories, workshops, and communes, and there are two
farms near the campus for students specializing in agriculture. The Normal College also runs a May 7th Cadre
School for cadres, staff, and leading members of the college.

丁 淑 元     Ding Shu-yuan
            Chairman, Department of Chinese

高 元 白     Gao Yuan-bai
            Professor of Chinese

吴 士 勋     Wu Shi-xun
            Teacher, Department of Chinese

何 世 华     He Shi-hua
            Teacher, Department of Chinese

刘 学 林     Liu Xue-lin
            Teacher, Department of Chinese

迟   锋     Chi Feng
            Teacher, Department of Chinese

李 吟 西     Li Yin-xi
            Teacher, Department of English

江 冰 华     Jiang Bing-hua
            Teacher, Department of English

宋 协 力     Song Xie-li
            Teacher, Department of English

<u>Yenan</u>          October 31 - November 2

张茂远          Zhang Mao-yuan

Deputy Director, Yenan District
Bureau of Education

孟兆彬          Meng Zhao-bin

Responsible Person, Yenan District
Office of Foreign Affairs

艾丕善          Ai Pei-shan

Staff Member, Yenan District Office
of Foreign Affairs

<u>Shanghai</u>     November 4 - 5, 8 - 9

<u>Shanghai Municipal Bureau of Education</u>

邹劍秋          Zou Jian-qiu

Responsible Person, Revolutionary
Committee

蒋福良          Jiang Fu-liang

Staff Member, Revolutionary Committee

何    净          He Jing

Staff Member, Revolutionary Committee

凌永康          Ling Yong-kang

Staff Member, Revolutionary Committee

熊振华          Xiong Zhen-hua

Staff Member, Revolutionary Committee

娄有源          Lou You-yuan

Staff Member, Revolutionary Committee

黄明心          Huang Ming-xin

Staff Member, Revolutionary Committee

Monday, November 4

## Fudan University 复旦大学

Fudan is a comprehensive university of arts and sciences, founded in 1905. There are thirteen departments--seven of liberal arts and six of natural sciences: 1) Chinese language, 2) history, 3) philosophy, 4) economics, 5) journalism, 6) foreign languages, 7) international politics, 8) mathematics, 9) physics, 10) chemistry, 11) biology, 12) optics, and 13) atomic physics.

The university's enrollment is currently 3,500 students, of which approximately 3,000 come from worker-peasant-soldier backgrounds. The teaching staff numbers 1,800, including 157 professors and associate professors, 292 lecturers, and the rest assistants. The university also runs short-term training classes, lasting from several weeks to one year, for 5,000 students. Correspondence classes are provided for an additional 6,700 students.

Fudan operates some small factories, including an electronics factory, and optics factory, and a petroleum chemicals factory, and has links with more than eighty factories and communes in the Shanghai area.

郑 绍 良　　Zheng Shao-liang

Responsible Person, Educational Revolution Group

许 宝 华　　Xu Bao-hua

Department of Chinese, Chinese Language Educational Group

李 振 麟　　Li Zhen-lin

Professor, Chinese Department (lexicography)

胡 裕 树　　Hu Yu-shu

Professor, Chinese Department (host/escort while in Shanghai)

吴 文 淇
Wu Wen-qi
Professor, Chinese Department

刘 大 杰
Liu Da-jie
Professor, Chinese Department
(literature)

邓 明 以
Deng Ming-yi
Teacher, Chinese Department

范 晓
Fan Xiao
Teacher, Chinese Department

叶 易
Ye Yi
Teacher, Chinese Department

薛 诗 绮
Xue Shi-qi
Teacher, Foreign Languages
Department (English-Chinese dictionary)

雷 烈 江
Lei Lie-jiang
Teacher, Foreign Languages
Department (English-Chinese dictionary)

孙 铢
Sun Zhu
Teacher, Foreign Languages
Department

朱 德 逵
Zhu De-kui
Teacher, Foreign Languages
Department

冯 善 萍
Feng Shan-ping
Teacher, Foreign Languages
Department

Tuesday, November 5

<u>Shanghai School for the Deaf</u>

樂　平　　Le Ping (f.)
　　　　　Leading Member, Revolutionary
　　　　　Committee

朱 庭 华　Zhu Ting-hua
　　　　　Workers' Propaganda Team

芦 美 银　Lu Mei-yin
　　　　　Member, Revolutionary Committee

许　　　　Dr. Xu
　　　　　PLA doctor

Thursday, November 7

<u>Suzhou</u>

张 友 聚　Zhang You-ju
　　　　　Bureau of Education

肖 振 声　Xiao Zhen-sheng
　　　　　Bureau of Education

朱 中 浩　Zhu Zhong-hao
　　　　　Foreign Affairs Group

卢 文 保　Lu Wen-bao
　　　　　Foreign Affairs Group

沈 仲 辉　Shen Zhong-hui
　　　　　Foreign Affairs Group

沈 受 章　Shen Shou-zhang
　　　　　Foreign Affairs Group

胡 方 石     Hu Fang-shi
            Sandalwood fan factory

钱 淑 谕     Qian Shu-yu
            Institute of Embroidery

Friday, November 8 - a.m.

## Shanghai Normal University

Shanghai Normal University was founded in 1951 to train middle school teachers. There are currently 2,000 teachers and 7,000 students in twelve departments: 1) education and pedagogy, 2) Chinese language, 3) history, 4) political education, 5) foreign languages (English, Russian, French, German, Japanese), 6) physics, 7) chemistry, 8) mathematics, 9) geology, 10) biology, 11) literature and art, and 12) physical culture. In addition to these departments, there are three research groups: 1) foreign education, 2) foreign geography, and 3) river mouth, estuary, and coast-line research.

The Chinese Language Department has enrolled three classes of students since the Cultural Revolution. The first class, numbering 109 students, has already graduated, leaving 400 students in the first and second-year level. By the end of November 1974, the Chinese Language Department expects to have 850 students. There are 200 faculty members in the department.

The Foreign Languages Department includes 510 students, of which 360 are studying English, 310 teachers and sixty staff members.

Shanghai Normal University also provides advanced study for middle school teachers and spare-time study for people who are currently teaching.

Zhang Tian-zhou

Leading Member of Educational Revolution Group

Zuo Huan-qi

English teacher

Chen Jian

Teacher, Foreign Languages Department

Gang Yi-feng

Teacher, Foreign Language Department
(in charge of English broadcasting)

Gu Yi

Department of Chinese

Yao Li-yuan

Department of Chinese

Tang Yi-zai

Department of Chinese   ·

Yan Yi-ming

Department of Chinese

Zan Gui-fen

Pedagogy Department
(Middle School language teaching)


Yuan Yin-guang


Chen Shao-yi

Research student

Friday, November 8 - p.m.

<u>Shanghai Foreign Language Institute</u>

When the Institute was founded in December 1949, only
one language was taught: Russian.  By the Cultural Revolution the number of languages had increased to seven and
by 1974, to ten: Russian, English, German, French, Arabic,
Spanish, Japanese, Italian, Greek, and Albanian.  The six
courses taught to each class are politics, foreign language,

physical education, Chinese, the geography, history, and economics of the selected country, and a second foreign language.

The enrollment is now 1,685 students. The largest percentage studies English; then follow French, German, Japanese, Spanish, and Arabic.

蔡 增 良  Cai Zeng-liang
Responsible Person, Educational Revolution Group

孙 宗 仰  Sun Zong-yang
Responsible Person, Teaching Group of Educational Revolution

徐 金 玉  Xu Jin-yu
Responsible Person, Revolutionary Committee of Department of English

秦 小 孟  Qin Xiao-meng
Vice-Chairman, Revolutionary Committee of Department of English

陆 佩 玄  Lu Pei-xuan
Associate Professor, Department of English

林 钧 裘  Lin Jun-qiu
Chairman, Audio-Visual Lab

吴 在 拍  Wu Zai-pai
Responsible Person, Audio-Visual Center

张 正 邦  Zhang Zheng-bang
Teacher, Department of English (Interpreter)

于　晶　Yu Jing
Worker-peasant-soldier student

黄　明　Huang Ming
Worker-peasant-soldier student

李 良 海　Li Liang-hai
Worker-peasant-soldier student

Friday evening at hotel

Fudan University participants

朱 建 新　Zhu Jian-xin
Teacher of English, Foreign
Language Department

陆 国 强　Lu Guo-qiang
Teacher of English, Foreign
Language Department

孙　铢　Sun Zhu
Third-year student of English

冯 善 蓬　Feng Shan-peng
Third-year student of English

November 10 - 12

Canton

Lin Chuan
Vice-Director, Provincial Bureau
of Education

Gao Hua-nian
Professor, Department of Chinese,
Zhongshan University

Fang Shu-zhen

Professor, Department of Foreign
Languages, Zhongshan University

Wang Ping-shan

City Bureau of Education

Xu Wen-feng

Vice-Director, City Bureau of
Education

Gong Hua-ji

Foreign Language Institute

Chen Wu

Staff, Provincial Bureau of
Education

Bao Zong-heng

Staff, Provincial Bureau of
Education

Sun Yu

Staff, City Bureau of Education

Monday, November 11

## Zhongshan University 中 山 大 学

Formerly known as Guangdong University, this university
was renamed in 1926, two years after its founding, to
commemorate Dr. Sun Yat-sen, who died in 1925.  Zhongshan
University has eleven departments: Chinese, history, philosophy, economics, foreign languages, biology, chemistry,
physics (electronics), metallurgy, mechanics, and dynamics.
There is also a department of library science.  The faculty numbers 1,000 and the students, 2,000.

Yang Yi-bai

Vice-Director, Group in charge of
educational reform

高 华 年　　Gao Hua-nian
　　　　　　Professor, Chinese Department

潘 允 中　　Pan Yun-zhong
　　　　　　Professor, Chinese Department

王　　起　　Wang Qi
　　　　　　Professor, Chinese Department

李 新 魁　　Li Xin-kui
　　　　　　Teacher, Chinese Department

冯 志 白　　Feng Zhi-bai
　　　　　　Teacher, Chinese Department

傅 雨 贤　　Fu Yü-xian
　　　　　　Teacher, Chinese Department

罗 伟 豪　　Lo Wei-hao
　　　　　　Teacher, Chinese Department

黄 家 教　　Huang Jia-jiao
　　　　　　Teacher, Chinese Department

张 振 林　　Zhang Zhen-lin
　　　　　　Teacher, Chinese Department

孙 稚 雏　　Sun Zhi-chu
　　　　　　Teacher, Chinese Department

余 伟 文　　Yu Wei-wen
　　　　　　Teacher, Chinese Department

方 淑 针　　Fang Shu-zhen
　　　　　　Professor, Department of
　　　　　　English

# NOTES ON CONTRIBUTORS

*Chin-chuan Cheng* is Associate Professor of Linguistics and Chinese at the University of Illinois in Urbana. Associate Editor of the <u>Journal of Chinese Linguistics</u>, he has published particularly on Chinese phonology, as in numerous articles and his book of 1973: <u>A Synchronic Phonology of Mandarin Chinese</u>.

*Charles A. Ferguson* is Professor of Linguistics at Stanford University. He has long concerned himself with problems of language reform, especially in India, Ethiopia and the Middle East. He has published widely in the field of sociolinguistics; some of his articles have been brought together in <u>Language Structure and Language Use</u>, 1971.

*Anne FitzGerald* is Professional Associate, Committee on Scholarly Communication with the People's Republic of China, National Academy of Sciences. A specialist on modern Chinese language and society, she was formerly a Political Assistant in the Department of State, and traveled to the PRC in April and May, 1972, with the Mansfield-Scott delegation.

*Victoria Fromkin* is Professor of Linguistics at the University of California in Los Angeles, and Chairman of the Department of Linguistics. She has specialized in phonological theory, experimental phonetics and neurolinguistics. Among her publications are <u>Speech Errors as Linguistic Evidence</u>, 1973, and the Development of Language in Genie: A Case of Language Acquisition Beyond the "Critical Period." <u>Brain and Language</u> 1, 81-107, 1974.

*William Labov* is Professor of Linguistics at the University of Pennsylvania. He has been especially concerned with processes of communication in the inner city, as in <u>The Social Stratification of English in New York City</u>, 1966, and <u>Language in the Inner City</u>, 1972. Besides his study of linguistic variation, he has dealt with patterns of language change in contemporary society.

*Winfred P. Lehmann* is Ashbel Smith Professor of Linguistics and Germanic Languages at the University of Texas at Austin. He has dealt especially with historical linguistics, as in Historical Linguistics: an Introduction, 2nd ed. 1973, and Proto-Indo-European Syntax, 1974.

*Anatole Lyovin* is Associate Professor of Linguistics in the University of Hawaii at Manoa. His special fields of interest are synchronic and diachronic phonology, particularly the phonology of Chinese dialects and comparative Sino-Tibetan. Besides publishing articles and reviews in these fields, he is co-author of Chinese Linguistics Bibliography on Computer, 1970.

*John B. Lum* is Senior Associate with the Multicultural Task Force of the National Institute of Education. Formerly a Research Assistant with the San Francisco Unified School District, he has specialized in Asian-American concerns and studies, bilingual and multicultural education and in political systems analysis and educational politics.

*Frederick W. Mote* is Professor of Chinese History in the East Asian Studies Department of Princeton University. Among his publications are Japanese-Sponsored Governments in China, 1937-1945, 1954, The Poet Kao Ch'i, 1336-1374, 1962, and Intellectual Foundations of China, 1971.

*Jerry Norman* is Associate Professor of Chinese Language and Linguistics at the University of Washington in Seattle. His primary fields of interest are Chinese language and dialects, Chinese historical linguistics, Altaic and Manchu linguistics. Among his recent articles is The Initials of Proto-Min, Journal of Chinese Linguistics, 2.27-36, 1974.

*Howard E. Sollenberger* is Director of the Foreign Service Institute, Department of State. Earlier a professor of Chinese Studies with the Foreign Service Institute, and dean of its School of Languages, he is especially interested in Chinese language and area studies, and in training and orientation for personnel assigned to overseas service.

*James J. Wrenn* is Professor of Linguistics at Brown University. His special fields of interest are the application of computer techniques to the processing of Chinese texts for textual studies, with an aim to the development of teaching aids, as well as language teaching methodology and programmed learning in Chinese. Among his publications is Chinese Language Teaching in the United States: The State of the Art, 1968.